Y0-EJL-143

WITHDRAWN

Alexandria Public Library
HARTFORD PUBLIC LIBRARY
Alexandria, Ohio

LIPREADING

For the Oral Deaf and Hard-of-Hearing Person

LIPREADING
For the Oral Deaf and Hard-of-Hearing Person

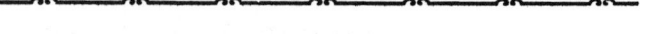

By

ELIZABETH HAZARD

CHARLES C THOMAS • PUBLISHER
Springfield • *Illinois* • *U.S.A.*

Published and Distributed Throughout the World by
CHARLES C THOMAS • PUBLISHER
BANNERSTONE HOUSE
301–327 East Lawrence Avenue, Springfield, Illinois, U.S.A.
NATCHEZ PLANTATION HOUSE
735 North Atlantic Boulevard, Fort Lauderdale, Florida, U.S.A.

This book is protected by copyright. No part of it may be reproduced in any manner without written permission from the publisher.

© 1971, by CHARLES C THOMAS • PUBLISHER
Library of Congress Catalog Card Number: 71-157285

With THOMAS BOOKS *careful attention is given to all details of manufacturing and design. It is the Publisher's desire to present books that are satisfactory as to their physical qualities and artistic possibilities and appropriate for their particular use.* THOMAS BOOKS *will be true to those laws of quality that assure a good name and good will.*

Printed in the United States of America
BB-14

To Adele B. Gordon

my friend and teacher

PREFACE

This book is the result of my search for material to use in teaching my hard-of-hearing and deafened pupils to lipread. Today there is little in the way of lessons that can be passed on to the student as work to be practiced both at home and with the teacher.

It is my belief that synthesizing is the only practical method of using lipreading. Synthesis is the goal of the competent lipreader. However, to achieve it, much analytical study must precede it. Vowels and syllables are the most important part of teaching a student what to look for in learning this technique. I have, therefore, emphasized practice work on vowels and on syllables. The more syllables a person can learn to recognize, the more quickly he can grasp the words.

The book contains syllable and syllable drills together with word drills and word comparisons. These exercises may be given to the pupil for home practice. The sentences that accompany each lesson have a two-fold purpose. One is to familiarize the student with the words and syllables he has practiced at home. The second purpose is to give him practice in synthesis and the rhythm of natural speech.

I have also included material which I, as a deaf teacher, myself dependent on lipreading, have found to be stumbling blocks in my ability to lipread. I have also noted that my pupils have consistently had difficulty in the same areas of comprehension, notably with words beginning with a vowel or diphthong. I have also found that more attention and practice must be given to word endings.

I have written these lessons for teaching lipreading to hard-of-hearing and deafened persons who have speech and a memory of the rhythm of speech.

Elizabeth Hazard

TO THE TEACHER

The following lessons which I have written for teaching lipreading to hard-of-hearing and deafened oral adults have served me as a good basic or fundamental method of teaching my pupils to lipread. I do not believe there to be any quick and easy way to learn this art, and I never allow my students to think that it will be quick and easy. Lipreading is presumably a talent that they are in great need of developing if they are to continue to be able to communicate with other people; thus it is better that they face the difficulties of learning at the outset and so not become disillusioned and discouraged after a few lessons.

Most beginners ask me how long it will take them to learn to lipread and how many lessons they will need. I tell them that it is impossible to answer as the ability to learn differs with each individual; some people can learn more quickly and easily than others. We must, therefore, continue to work until the pupil can read well enough both from the front face and in profile for lipreading to be an asset to him in the communication of everyday life.

I want to point out, especially to those teachers newly entering the field, that teaching an oral deaf or hard-of-hearing person to lipread is a very different procedure from teaching children who were born deaf to speak and to lipread.

The oral deaf have learned to speak before they lost their hearing. They have the memory of the sound and rhythm of speech. They have the vocabulary and grammar commensurate with their education and environment. You are not, therefore, called upon to teach them to speak nor to correct their grammar. If, when you give them a sentence, they repeat it to you in poor English, accept the rendition, provided that the sense of what was said is not altered. The important thing is that they understand what is said to them and can communicate with people in whatever environment they are accustomed to. You are teaching them to communicate and not giving them lessons in English.

Teacher's Voice Volume

The hearing problems of each person must be gone over thoroughly; by this I mean—has the pupil been totally deafened, can he or she wear a hearing aid and if not, why not; if he is wearing an aid or aids, how much help it is giving him. Always experiment with each student to find the appropriate level of loudness which you are going to use in speaking to them. In the case of a person who has some hearing left and does not wear an aid, the teacher's voice should be pitched just low enough so that the pupil can hear the teacher's voice, but not sufficiently to be able to understand the words; he must have to reach for the sound and interpret it by what he sees. The same system is to be used with the student wearing a hearing aid; he must be taught to coordinate the help he is getting from his aid with lipreading. Never give lipreading without any voice. If the student has become totally deafened or has a hearing loss so severe that an aid is of no help, then the normal speaking voice volume should be used.

Reduction of Tension

Study each pupil carefully so that you are in a position to give him the maximum help. Much depends on the age of the person being taught, his psychological and emotional characteristics. Watch for nervousness, tension and pressure. Most hard-of-hearing people suffer from tension; the nature of their handicap makes it almost inevitable. However, you can help to decrease this tension while giving the lesson. When you see the pupil's tension building up, due to the necessity for extreme concentration, try to ease this pressure by telling the student to relax for a few minutes and let him unwind. This is a good moment to talk to the student about tension, pressure and fatigue, and their effects on the lipreader. Explain to him that the more tense he becomes, the more difficult it is to lipread; also make him aware of the fact that fatigue will be likely to affect his ability to lipread too. This is normal among people learning to lipread, and he must not allow himself to become discouraged by tension and fatigue. Impress on him that by relaxing, he will help himself most.

Introduction of Lesson

In the first lesson tell the pupil that lipreading is phonetics, and that from now on he must think in terms of the shape of the sound that is being spoken, instead of thinking in terms of the letters of the alphabet and the way words are spelled. At all times, discourage the student from asking, when he misses a word, "Does it begin with s or t or d?"

Always make certain that the pupil has understood your instructions, especially in the beginning; if there is any doubt as to whether or not he has understood you, write out for him what you want him to know. Likewise, when you are giving him a relaxing moment, write what you are telling him if he cannot understand when you raise your voice to a normal level.

Scheduling of Lessons

I find the best schedule for lipreading lessons to be one-half hour twice a week; one hour is too long a period for total concentration and does more harm than good to the pupil through fatigue and discouragement. Also, lessons twice a week give the pupil time in between to practice the homework.

Work at Home

It is very necessary to impress on the student the need for conscientious daily practice of the homework assigned to him. This practice is essential; unless the pupil is made to understand this and agrees to comply in this matter, he may as well give up any idea of becoming a lipreader.

The homework practice should be done, if possible, in two phases. First, the lipreader should practice the exercises in front of the mirror, watching himself say the drills and words, not only observing how they look on his own mouth and face, but also noticing how they feel on his mouth, tongue and lips when he says them. The latter can be of great help if the pupil is unable to understand a word; making the same movements of the lips and tongue as he sees the teacher doing can often bring the pupil recognition of the word. The second phase of the practice should be done with a member of the family or a friend who will say the drills and words for him to lipread. It is better to practice for short periods of ten or fifteen minutes three or four times a day than to practice for a longer time only once a day. In some cases you will find that the well-meaning relative or friend decides it would be better to practice something other than the prescribed material and give it without voice; in such cases it is well to let the student know that the homework you have given has a purpose, and no other material or manner of giving it is to be substituted.

Synthesizing

Also explain to your student that only 25 percent of what is said can be seen, and therefore it is necessary to synthesize; or in terms more understandable to the pupil, he must discover what the subject being talked about is by picking out the key words and as many others as he is able to see, thus putting together the sense and meaning of what has been said. A student should be trained not to stop lipreading if he misses the first part of what was said, as the subsequent words may enable him to reconstruct what had gone before.

In explaining the above, it is helpful to take a paragraph in a book or paper and show the student how many words can be eliminated and still retain the sense of the subject.

If, in trying to lipread a sentence, the pupil has managed to get only a few words of the sentence but not enough to make sense out of it, ask him what he thinks he has read and write down these words for him with the requisite number of dashes between the words to represent the words he has not understood. This helps him to visualize the shape and rhythm of the sentence. Having done this, give him the sentence again and see if he can add anything to the words he has already perceived. In the beginning it may be necessary to repeat the sentence several times, each time adding more words to fill the gaps until the lipreader has understood the sentence. This helps to train the student's power of filling in the gaps, and with practice he learns to synthesize.

I feel that syllables and syllable drills are a very important aid in learning to lipread. All sentences are made up of syllables forming words, and the more syllables a pupil can learn to recognize, the more easily and quickly the words will come to him. These drills should be given as rapidly as the pupil can recognize them, obviously in the beginning the pace will be slow, but as the student progresses speed up the syllable drills accordingly.

In giving out a lesson as homework, explain the contents of the lesson carefully to the pupil. Give him a description of the shape of the sound to be practiced and its characteristics; go over the syllables and syllable drills with him to be sure he understands the correct pronunciation of each syllable and the meaning of the diacritical markings used. Also go through the words in case there are any with which he is unfamiliar.

When giving the lesson that the student has practiced at home, first take the syllables, then the syllable drills, followed by the words. Explain to the pupil, if he misses some words, that they will be more recognizable when they are given in a sentence. Next give the sentences for the particular lesson being studied. The whole lesson, of course, being given with voice volume just below the student's threshold of speech comprehension.

If the pupil has difficulty with the lesson, do not be afraid to have him repeat the lesson, explain to him that it is better to have a good comprehension of the shape of the sound being studied before going on to the next lesson and there is no disgrace attached to repeating a lesson; most people have to, especially in the sounds that are most difficult, such as T—d—n, k and hard c and hard g. Never let the student feel that a lesson must be rushed through in order to go on to the next. A relaxed atmosphere must be maintained at all times to prevent the pupil from building up tension. Each lesson has been structured to fill a half-hour lipreading session at the pace of an average student.

To go back for a moment to synthesization in lipreading, the question comes up: how much deviance from the sentence given is acceptable? In the early stages, I think the pupil should stick as closely as possible to a verbatim rendering, as the teacher is giving sentences which include the specific words from a particular lesson which the pupil has studied and must learn to lipread. When the student is fairly well along in the technique of lipreading, then more variance is allowable, so long as the meaning of what has been said is not altered. This freer interpretation will, of course, speed up the pupil's lipreading, but synthesization must be thought of as a goal and not the means to an end, namely learning to lipread.

I want to here mention my reason for including the sound of short o and y with the sounds of you, yer and ior. The short o is often omitted in the newer editions of some lipreading lesson books, due to the fact that in so many words spelled with a short o, the o takes the sound aw or ah; however, there are still enough words with the true sound of short o that I feel it should not be omitted. I have also included y as in you, yer and ior which also of late has been omitted and with which I found many pupils having difficulty.

While teaching I have been, shall I say, keeping score of the words which pupils seem to miss the most often. Words beginning with a vowel appear with the most frequency. I think this is due to the fact that there are fewer words beginning with a vowel than with a consonant, so the student gets in the habit of looking for a consonant at the beginning of a word. The student should be made more aware of words beginning with a vowel. I have, therefore, included twelve lessons on words beginning with a vowel or a diphthong.

I found words endings to be another area of uncertainty and have included twenty lessons on word ending combinations.

Homophenous sounds and words must, of course, be explained to the pupil, but in teaching I do not put too much stress on them, as 50 percent of our words when spoken look alike on the lips, and to call too much attention to this fact, I feel, will only confuse the student by giving him the added burden of continually watching for them; this distracts him in his efforts to lipread.

Reading a short story to the pupil and having him tell you in his own words what the story was about is good practice in developing synthetic lipreading. I do not think it should be undertaken until the pupil has become a passable lipreader with a good foundation in all sounds of speech, particularly the vowels, and is ready to speed up his lipreading by synthesizing. If undertaken before, it necessitates too much concentration for too long a period and is apt to confuse and discourage the student.

I have used these lessons successfully with pupils from the age of twelve years up. I personally do not favor teaching hard-of-hearing people in groups or classes as their hearing losses are too disparate, likewise their learning abilities. Therefore, I have not used these lessons in classes; however, the teacher may do so at his discretion. After all, a lipreading lesson book is only an aid to the teacher who must interpret it and use or alter the material to suit the needs of the pupils being taught. If the sentences are found to be too long, the teacher can shorten and adapt them. Occasionally a student will be found who is confused by the syllable drills, in which case the drills may be omitted and only the word drill given for practice at home. I would not advise, however, omitting the drills unless absolutely necessary. The adaptations made are up to each teacher's judgment.

I have numbered the sentences in the lessons and placed them in groups of four for the benefit of any teacher, who, like myself, is deaf and must lipread his pupils, which necessitates constant looking away from the book and back again. This makes keeping the place in the lesson much easier and avoids repetition of sentences already given to the student.

ACKNOWLEDGMENTS

My appreciation and thanks go to the following people:

Mrs. Adele B. Gordon and Mrs. Sandra C. Holley for their fine job of editing the book.

Mrs. Mary Haney, Supervisor of Teachers, New York School for the Deaf, White Plains, N.Y., for her encouragement and the loan of material.

Mrs. Jeanne Buynak for organization of material and for a very excellent job of manuscript typing.

E.H.

CONTENTS

	Page
Preface	vii
To the Teacher	ix
Acknowledgments	xvii

Lesson

THE SHAPE OF THE SOUND OF

1.	p, b, m and ah	3
2.	f, v and ō	6
3.	s, z, Soft c and ū–o͞o	9
4.	Short o͝o	12
5.	ā and th	15
6.	Long ē and sh	18
7.	wh and w	21
8.	aw and Hard g	24
9.	ou–ow	27
10.	Long ī	30
11.	oi–oy	33
12.	k and Hard c	36
13.	Short ă	39
14.	Short ĭ–y	42
15.	Short ŭ and h Before a Vowel	45
16.	Short ĕ and l	48
17.	Short ŏ and ch	51
18.	Vowel Sound of er–ir–ur	54
19.	r Before and After a Vowel	57
20.	n Before and After a Vowel	60
21.	y as in You and Words Ending in yer, ior	63
22.	d and t	66
23.	j and Soft g	69

Lesson

	Page
24. r After f, b, p and th	72
25. r After Hard c and Hard g	75
26. l After f, s, b and p	78
27. l After Hard c and g	81
28. dr and tr	84
29. sm, sp and sw Before a Vowel	87
30. st, sk and sc (hard c) Before a Vowel	90
31. str, scr and spr Before a Vowel	93
32. sl and sn Before a Vowel	96
33. q and sq Before a Vowel	99

WORDS BEGINNING WITH A VOWEL OR DIPHTHONG

34. Long ā	105
35. Long ō	108
36. Long ē	111
37. Long ī	114
38. Long ū–ōō–yōō–eū	117
39. ah	120
40. aw	123
41. Short ă	126
42. Short ĕ	129
43. Short ĭ	132
44. Short ŭ	135
45. er—ou—oi	138

WORDS ENDING WITH

46. s, x and z	141
47. sh, ch and ge	144
48. t and ed After b, f, v, s, m, p and gh	147
49. t and ed After r, l, c and ck	150
50. nd and nt	153
51. ng and nk	156
52. tch, ch With the Sound of tch and dge	159

Lesson	Page
53. ing and ic	162
54. ck After Short Vowels and ke After Long Vowels	165
55. nse and nce	168
56. ve and f, gh and ph With the Sound of f	171
57. y With the Sound of ĭ	174
58. l and ble	177
59. ion—(sh)ion	180
60. er—or—ar	183
61. less and ness	186
62. ful	189
63. ld and lt	192
64. st and ft	195
65. us and ous	198
Homophenous Sounds	203
Homophenous Words	203
Review of Pronouns, Verbs and Adverbs	205

LIPREADING

For the Oral Deaf and Hard-of-Hearing Person

LESSON 1

The Shape of the Sound of p, b, m and ah

p, b, m—look alike on the lips
   The lips open from a closed position.

ah—as in part
   The lips are relaxed forming a wide opening.
   The jaw drops.

ah and *p, b, m*

Syllable Drill:

        pah—bah—mah

Word Drill:

part	patch
mark	moon
palm	book
marble	band
march	mile
meet	pound
bell	paid
parch	park
ball	bark
barn	mail
best	back
boy	path
barber	partner

1. I will walk part of the way home with you.
2. Can you read my palm?
3. This hot sun will parch the ground.
4. We have a strawberry patch in the yard.

5. The school bell will ring soon.
6. Who do you think is best suited for the job?
7. Do you watch the ball games on TV?
8. Will you please take my book back to the library?
9. Please mark the place in the book that you want me to read.
10. The table has a white marble top.
11. Will you march in the Fourth of July parade?
12. Do come over and meet my friends.
13. If anybody comes in the yard, my dog will bark.
14. We live near a beautiful park.
15. I am going out to mail my letter.
16. There is a big red barn on my brother's farm.
17. When you go to the store, will you get me a pound of butter?
18. I have paid all my debts.
19. The path through the woods was covered with pine needles.
20. My law partner will handle your affairs.
21. My back aches from spading the ground.
22. The band played a lively march and everyone cheered.
23. The boy rode his bicycle to school.
24. He went to the barber to get his hair cut.
25. We are going for a moonlight sail tonight.
26. It is only a mile and a half to the school.
27. The soldiers were tired from the long march.
28. Will you mark the pattern for me to cut out?
29. The bark of a birch tree is white.
30. We are having a barn dance tomorrow.
31. I am going to park the car and will join you.
32. What time does the mail usually arrive?
33. I cannot make a straight part in my hair.
34. Palm trees grow in Florida.
35. My throat was parched after our long hot hike.
36. Do you want me to patch the elbow of your jacket?
37. The boy batted the ball through the school window.
38. How many books do you think you read in a year?
39. I will call you when we get back from our vacation.
40. I thought I heard the door bell ring.

Lesson 1

41. When you were a boy did you shoot marbles?
42. How many miles is it from here to Boston?
43. I always make a wish on the new moon.
44. I am going to meet my sister's train at 4:30.
45. The barber gave me a haircut and shave.
46. Who is your partner in business?
47. March can be such a windy and cold month.
48. You must mail your Christmas cards early.

LESSON 2

The Shape of the Sound of f, v and ō

f and v—look alike
The upper teeth touch the lower lip; the lips are not closed as for p, b, and m.

ō—as in vote
There is a puckered forward movement of the lips followed by a backward relaxed motion as the consonant to follow takes shape.

ō and f, v

Syllable Drill:

fah—fō	pah-mō
fō—bah	pō—fah
bah—vō	fō—mah
vō—mah	fō—fah

Word Drill:

poll	farm	bore
foot	force	life
vote	fare	wore
fine	sold	view
both	voice	pour
fade	sole	fall
rose	form	toast
vain	loaf	half
road	fire	phone
fold	boat	most
four	more	pose
few	coat	foam
vast	very	vacant

Lesson 2

1. Will you have buttered toast with your coffee?
2. The road was full of holes after the winter storms.
3. I sold my car and got a new station wagon.
4. He wore a blue suit to the dinner.
5. My feet are sore and I am weary from shopping.
6. It is a fine day for a long drive in the country.
7. The material was cheap and I am afraid it will fade.
8. The farm looked well cared for and prosperous.
9. Everyone should vote in an election.
10. I looked in vain for my book.
11. Please keep your voice low when talking.
12. The view of the mountains was breathtaking.
13. Both girls like winter sports.
14. The rose is one of my favorite flowers.
15. The boy is his sole relative.
16. Do sit down; I will pour you some coffee.
17. I will not force you to go with me.
18. How much is the railroad fare to Baltimore?
19. Did you hear the fire engines passing the house?
20. It is nice to go for a walk in the crisp fall air.
21. The university has a vast auditorium.
22. It is very kind of you to have gone to so much trouble.
23. There are several apartments vacant in the building.
24. His viewpoint is different from mine.
25. The polls will be open at eight o'clock.
26. I went to the store for a loaf of rye bread.
27. The woman was such a bore nobody would go near her.
28. We will pick you up at four o'clock.
29. I will phone you if I get any news.
30. I would like to buy half a watermelon.
31. I had the time of my life on the cruise.
32. That man has loafed all his life.
33. Most people enjoy watching television.
34. We waited for him to voice an opinion.
35. We all voted to have a barn dance.
36. The view was very vast and rather awesome.

37. Please fold these letters and put them in the envelopes.
38. There are only a few days left for Christmas shopping.
39. Have you ever found a four leaf clover?
40. I will take you fishing in my boat.
41. We had to force an entry because the door was locked.
42. The flowers were more than a foot tall.
43. Please fill out this form and sign it.
44. Yesterday afternoon it poured.
45. Do take off your coat, it's so warm in here.
46. Would you like to have some more ice cream?
47. My new car has foam rubber seats.
48. Did you pose for this picture?

LESSON 3

The Shape of the Sound of
s, z, Soft c and ū—ōō

s, z, soft c—look alike

The teeth are brought close together and the lips slightly parted.

ū–ōō—as in moon

The lips are drawn forward and puckered, the opening of the lips very small.

ū-ōō and s, z, soft c

Syllable Drill:

fah–fō–fōō   vah–vō–vōō
sah–sō–sōō   zah–zō–zōō
sō–fah–sō–sōō   bah–bō–bōō
mah–mōō–pō–pōō

Word Drill:

soup	pool	boom
saw	fool	loom
soap	rule	lose
move	food	soon
moon	boost	boot
mood	zoo	suit
sue	zodiac	piece
zither	zone	seem
sea	cease	sieze
paste	waste	taste

1. Everyone likes hot soup on a cold day.
2. I saw some old friends yesterday.
3. Do you listen to the soap operas on television?
4. We will move to our new house next week.

5. I always make a wish on the new moon.
6. Do you feel in the mood for a walk?
7. Mary is going to sue for divorce.
8. I wish I knew how to play the zither.
9. The sea is very rough today and the waves are high.
10. I am going to paste some pictures in my scrap book.
11. Do you have a swimming pool at your home?
12. I felt a fool not knowing the answer.
13. Silence is the rule of the library.
14. The price of food is awfully high.
15. The good news gave my morale a boost.
16. My brother takes the children to the zoo on Saturdays.
17. Do you know what sign of the zodiac you were born under?
18. What is the zip code number of your postal zone?
19. Everybody wishes the war would cease.
20. It is too bad to waste a beautiful day indoors.
21. Have you ever heard a sonic boom?
22. I have a loom and am learning to weave.
23. The doctor said he must lose more weight.
24. We will soon go back on standard time.
25. I lost a boot out of my shoe bag.
26. You will have to have the suit pressed. It is very wrinkled.
27. May I have another piece of bread please?
28. Let's seize our opportunity to go to the fair.
29. I seem to remember having read the book.
30. What kind of soup will you have for lunch?
31. Let me have a taste of your cake.
32. In the old days people used to make their own soap.
33. Will you help me move this bureau?
34. The clouds have loomed up and we can't see the moon.
35. The city is having a real estate boom.
36. As a rule I go to the market twice a week.
37. The food tasted good after our long hike.
38. We will pool our expenses on the trip across the country.
39. Please don't try to fool me.
40. I don't know what the rule is on borrowing books.

Lesson 3

41. I will get you some paste at the paper store.
42. It doesn't suit me to wear earrings.
43. The moonlight on the sea is very romantic.
44. Some good soup will give the invalid strength.
45. I have set up my loom to weave a rug.
46. When you visit the zoo, do you feed the elephant?
47. I bought several cakes of soap at the drug store.
48. Goodbye, I will see you again soon.

LESSON 4

The Shape of the Sound of Short o͝o

o͝o—*as in book*
This sound is more relaxed than ōo and there is a medium opening of the lips.

Short o͝o

Syllables:

po͝o—fo͝o—so͝o—bo͝o

Syllable Drill:

bah bo͝o	fah fō fo͝o
bah bō	bah bō bo͝o
fah po͝o	sah sō so͝o
bo͝o bōo so͝o so͞o	fo͝o fo͝o

Word Drill:

good	took
pull	forsook
full	should
wood	would
shook	push
look	cushion
bush	bull
wool	could
foot	hook
put	book
wolf	stood
cook	soot

1. The good news made us all happy.
2. You will need to have some pull to get the job.
3. The train was so full many people were standing.
4. What does a cord of wood cost now?

Lesson 4

5. We shook the tree to make the apples fall.
6. Will you look and see if my keys are on the table?
7. The bird has built a nest in the bush by the door.
8. My new coat is pure wool and very warm and light.
9. Don't let the beggar put his foot in the door.
10. Put all your papers away in the drawer.
11. That family has a hard time keeping the wolf from the door.
12. The cook is asking for another raise in wages.
13. I took the train because the weather was so bad for driving.
14. The woman forsook her husband and child.
15. I think I shall look for a cheaper apartment.
16. I am going to the movies. Would you care to go with me?
17. Push your chair nearer the fire where it is good and warm.
18. I bought a foam rubber cushion for my sofa.
19. We had better take the bull by the horns and get the job over.
20. I'd go with you if I could.
21. Hang your coat on the hook behind the door.
22. His last book was his best, I think.
23. It was raining so hard, I stood in a doorway to wait for the bus.
24. The stovepipe needs cleaning; it is full of soot.
25. It is a good thing I remembered to close the windows.
26. Which lever will you pull when you vote?
27. I felt full of misgivings about the plan.
28. The wood of the paneling is beautiful and in good condition.
29. I shook with fright when I saw the accident happen.
30. I will look for you at the meeting.
31. A bird in the hand is worth two in the bush.
32. I bought eight skeins of wool to make a sweater.
33. Do you enjoy going to football games?
34. I will put you in touch with a man who I think can help you.
35. He has cried wolf so often, no one pays attention to him.
36. Are you going to cook a turkey for Thanksgiving?
37. The work took far longer than I thought it was going to.
38. I forsook my earlier plans and I am glad I did.
39. Who do you think should head the committee?

40. Would there be any chance of your coming to town next week?
41. Please push the button to bring the elevator down.
42. In most cars they cushion the dashboard now.
43. My brother showed his prize bull at the fair.
44. Could I ask you to do me a favor?
45. I must pin the hooks on the draperies.
46. I went to get another book at the library.
47. The best man stood beside the groom.
48. If you open the window in the train you will get covered with soot.

LESSON 5

The Shape of the Sound of Long ā and th

ā—as in bake
　A downward movement of the jaw is very visible, the lips form a medium opening and are relaxed.

th—as in that
　The tip of the tongue is visible between the teeth or just back of the upper teeth. Lips slightly open.

Syllable Drill:

　　　　thō—thah—thā—sā—sō
　　　　mōō—mah—mā—fōō—fah—fā
　　　　thā—mā—sā—sō

Word Drill:

they	mail	same
bathe	face	chain
page	way	make
the	rain	fame
though	safe	race
seeth	lame	cape
name	thief	wave
faith	lathe	teeth
those	there	date
fair	say	may
sale	pair	pay

1. They think they will go with us tomorrow.
2. I will bathe the wound and clean it for you.
3. The story is on page eight of the evening paper.
4. The cups are on the second shelf.

5. The weather is lovely, though they say it will rain tonight.
6. Such insults are enough to make one's blood seethe.
7. My name is not in the telephone book.
8. I have faith in his management of the affair.
9. Those are the books I want to take with me.
10. I am going to bake a cake for the church fair.
11. The store is having a January white sale.
12. I want to mail this letter as soon as possible.
13. Does your face hurt from your sunburn?
14. Which way was the man running?
15. I would rather we had rain than snow.
16. It is not safe for the children to play in the street.
17. Jane is lame and walks with a limp.
18. They caught the thief with the money on him.
19. He says the lathe is broken and he can't finish the work.
20. Will you be able to finish the sweater before Christmas?
21. Please put the box over there in the corner.
22. Mary didn't say how long she will be away.
23. We live in the same street as your cousin.
24. They gave me a chain bracelet for my birthday.
25. Shall I make you some coffee or would you rather have tea?
26. His fame as a musician is world-wide.
27. I won fifty dollars in the third race.
28. We spent our vacation on the Cape this year.
29. An eight foot wave struck the boat.
30. She has beautiful teeth and a lovely smile.
31. I bought a pair of side tables at the auction.
32. My sister's boy is a Senate page.
33. Your next appointment is on what date?
34. If you bathe your face you won't look as though you cried.
35. Fame came to him at an early age.
36. The dog pulls so, I am not able to hold his chain.
37. What name have they given their new baby?
38. Neither race nor faith should enter into hiring a man for the job.
39. The mail is very late today.
40. She may stay over for a few more days.

41. I think I will get my cape. It is a little cool sitting out here.
42. A wave of indignation swept the crowd.
43. My opinion is the same as yours.
44. Did the doctor say how long Bill would be in the hospital?
45. How much did you have to pay for your new washing machine?
46. Will you take those packages to the Post Office for me?
47. As the day is fair, let's go to the beach.
48. I will take my raincoat, though I don't think it will rain.

LESSON 6

The Shape of the Sound of Long ē and sh

ē—as in seem
  The lips draw slightly back and the opening of the lips is narrow.

sh—as shame
  The lips thrust forward and the opening of the lips is rather square in shape.

sh and ē

Syllables:
  shē—shōō—shā—shō—shah
  mē—thē—sē—bē—fē—pē

Syllable Drill:
  fah—mē
  fah—mā
  shē—mā
  mā—shō
  shō—mē
  She may show me their beach.

Word Drill:

sharp	shake	these
show	shave	meat
shoe	feel	seed
shape	feast	fear
shame	seal	seat
sheep	beach	peep
she	peel	theme
sheet	mean	seem
shoot	beef	sheaf
sheen	veal	beans

Lesson 6

1. I have cut my finger on this sharp knife.
2. Please show me your lovely garden.
3. My shoe pinches and it hurts me to walk.
4. The oak tree has such a beautiful shape.
5. It is a shame that you had to miss the concert.
6. Sheep are such placid animals.
7. She is my father's sister.
8. Please give me a sheet of paper from your desk.
9. I have been trying to shoot a woodchuck all summer.
10. Will you shake the crumbs off this tablecloth for me?
11. The satin material has a nice sheen.
12. I don't feel much like working today.
13. On Thanksgiving we had a real feast.
14. I will seal my letter, then we will go and mail it.
15. It's so crowded on the beach you can't find a place to sit down.
16. Will you help me to peel these apples for the pie?
17. Excuse me, I didn't mean to interrupt what you were saying.
18. My favorite meat is beef, especially steak.
19. Men don't often go the barber to get a shave these days.
20. We always seed the lawn in the autumn.
21. In Italy they eat a great deal of veal.
22. I fear that my candidate is going to lose.
23. I couldn't get a seat on the train and had to stand all the way.
24. The price of meat is terrifically high these days.
25. I took a peep at the children in the dancing class.
26. What is the theme of his new novel?
27. I always seem to forget to do something.
28. The letter must be in that sheaf of papers on my desk.
29. I don't think I will go to the meeting either.
30. Do you enjoy pork and beans with brown bread?
31. This meat is so tough I really will need a sharp knife to carve it.
32. The shape of the seal is most unusual.
33. The baby bird gave a peep as his mother flew up with a worm in her beak.

34. He came to shake hands with me after the meeting.
35. I think it is a shame to shoot a graceful deer.
36. I don't mean to contradict you, but are you sure of that statement?
37. Fear is at the bottom of so much of the trouble.
38. Please peel off the back of this Band-aid for me.
39. The wood panel was well cared for and had a rich sheen.
40. She sent me three seats for the new play.
41. Some people think it lucky to find a horseshoe.
42. Will you have beef or lamb for dinner?
43. We will beach the boat and look for a place to picnic.
44. They had a very close shave when the tree fell near their car.
45. I must get some bird seed to feed the wild birds.
46. The thunder made the house shake.
47. I have a sharp stone in my shoe. I must get it out.
48. He must write a theme for his Spanish lesson.

LESSON 7

The Shape of the Sound of wh and w

wh and w—as in where or way

The lips have the same puckered forward movement as for ōō. The wh and w sounds come only before a vowel.

Syllables:

whā—whō—whah—whē—wōō—wā—wah—wō—wē

Syllable Drill:

shē mā sī	fah—wō
thā mā fī	hōō wō
wē mā bī	wē—wō
mā bī wŏŏ	wē—wā
bī whī wŏŏ	thā—wā
We may buy the white wool.	wā—wī
	They wait for his wife.

Word Drill:

woe	wave	when	wait
winter	weave	what	white
way	waif	where	wire
watch	wide	wood	wade
while	wheel	wife	wool
weed	want	weak	wore

Compare:

What was?	Where is?	Why is?
What is?	Where was?	Why were?
What were?	Where were?	Why was?

1. So much sadness and woe has befallen the world.
2. We are going to Spain next winter.
3. Which way should I go to reach the subway?
4. My watch has stopped. What time is it?

5. I will go to the pharmacy while you are finishing the work.
6. I always weed my garden when I want to think out a problem.
7. The huge wave nearly washed the man overboard.
8. The poor little waif looked starved.
9. I will weave a rug for my living room on my loom.
10. The old house has wide floor boards.
11. Wheel the patient into her room. I think she is tired.
12. What do you want me to give you for Christmas?
13. When is your next appointment with the doctor?
14. I will do whatever you think best.
15. My book is not where I left it. Who has taken it?
16. This wood is so dry, it burns very rapidly.
17. His wife had an operation last week.
18. The tea is too weak. It is like dishwater.
19. If you are in a hurry, don't wait for me.
20. The bridegroom wore a white carnation in his buttonhole.
21. I will send you a wire when I am ready to come home.
22. We had to wade through snow a foot deep to reach the car.
23. We got some wool at the new yarn shop.
24. Did your new shoes hurt you the first time you wore them?
25. What was the reason that she couldn't come today?
26. Where is the copper wire for hanging the picture?
27. Mary has been in the South all winter.
28. What is your opinion of the book?
29. Where was the parents' meeting held?
30. I don't know when I will be able to come into town again.
31. What was your opinion of the six speakers?
32. Did you ever try to do any woodcarving?
33. I am knitting some white wool socks for my niece.
34. Will you watch the hockey game on TV?
35. I must buy some chicken wire for my sweetpeas to climb on.
36. That is not the right way to pick up dropped stitches.
37. While I was waiting to be checked out at the supermarket, I saw Mary.

Lesson 7

38. It's easier to poison weeds in the driveway than to pull them out.
39. I think the stream is too wide to wade across.
40. The virus I had has left me feeling weak and washed out.
41. I waved to you and your wife at the game but you didn't see me.
42. What can we do to while away the time between trains?
43. Where was the poor little waif found?
44. He wore his hair very long and I thought it unbecoming to him.
45. Someone has borrowed my wheelbarrow and not returned it.
46. I will wait for you until three o'clock.
47. I don't want to put on any more weight.
48. Woe befall you if you do not practice your lesson.

LESSON 8

The Shape of the Sound of aw and Hard g

aw—as in saw and ball
   In the shape of the sound of aw the lips are slightly puckered and the opening of the lips rather round. Then the jaw drops slightly.

hard g—as in go and gate
   The sound of hard g has no shape. It is sometimes called a nasal sound. The movement takes place in the back of the throat and the air is expelled when making the sound; in some people a slight movement of the neck muscles may be seen. This sound must be usually realized by the context.

aw and hard g

Syllables:

paw—saw—faw—shaw—thaw—waw
gā—gah—gōō—gē—gō

Syllable Drill:

Thā gō	How gā	whī sō
Wē gō	How gī	whī saw
Wē saw	Wē gī	lī saw
Ī saw	Wē caw	Ī lī
I saw them go.	Ī caw	dōō lī
	caw cō	dōō yōō
	I caught a cold.	Do you like white sauce?

Word Drill:

fall	short	give
saw	lawn	get
ball	tall	good
raw	taught	gold
dawn	sauce	guilt

Lesson 8

walk	go	gone
wharf	game	guide
call	goat	guess
caught	gate	goad
bought	gay	geese

1. Be careful not to fall on these steep stairs.
2. If you want good exercise, saw wood.
3. We went to the inaugural ball.
4. It's awfully raw and windy today.
5. I never shut my eyes last night until nearly dawn.
6. Shall we go for a walk in the park?
7. We are going down to the wharf to try the fishing.
8. I am waiting for Andy to call me and tell me when he is coming.
9. I am afraid the children have caught colds.
10. We have bought a cottage on the seashore in New Jersey.
11. We are only going to make a short visit this year.
12. The bird bath on the lawn needs more water.
13. My nephew is very tall and he plays basketball.
14. Agnes taught the third grade for many years.
15. Do you like cranberry sauce with your turkey?
16. I will go with you as far as the bus stop.
17. What sport do you like best to watch?
18. Poor Ross! I am afraid they made him the scapegoat.
19. The gate is falling off its hinges. I must get it repaired.
20. It was a gay party and we didn't get home until nearly 4:30.
21. Please give me your word that it won't happen again.
22. I think I will get a new car in the spring.
23. As soon as we have good weather, I will clip the hedge.
24. The child received a gold locket for her birthday.
25. His guilt showed plainly on his face.
26. The firewood is all gone; I will chop some more.
27. In England a girl scout is called a girl guide.
28. Can you guess who I saw yesterday?
29. Would you care to play eighteen holes of golf on Saturday?
30. There was a little girl in charge of the flock of geese.

31. I always feel melancholy in the fall.
32. He cut the grass very short. I hope the sun won't burn up the lawn.
33. I caught the goat chewing my flowers.
34. Will you go to the game with Bill on Saturday?
35. Please give our good friend my regards.
36. I have decided to get Gordon a gold watch.
37. It never dawned on me what she meant to do.
38. Please close the gate so the geese won't get out.
39. Do you like to nibble on raw carrots?
40. The children were up at dawn on Christmas morning.
41. I have been writing short stories for a magazine.
42. Who taught you to drive a car?
43. I bought all new saucepans when I moved here.
44. Do you walk to work when the weather is not too raw?
45. I made a long distance call to my friend, but we only had a short talk.
46. What is your guess? Do you think the fellow guilty?
47. She tipped the guide when we left the museum.
48. May I give you some more chocolate sauce on your ice cream?

LESSON 9

The Shape of the Sound of
ou—ow

ou—ow—as in pound or town

The shape of this sound is the relaxed wide opening of ah followed rapidly by the forward puckered movement of ōo.

ou—ow

Syllables:

thou—bow—shou—fou—sou—pow

Syllable Drill:

fah—fou	shē—sē
hōo—fou	shē—sō
hōo—mou	thā—sō
thā—mou	thā—sī
thā—plou	thā—fī
mā—plou	hōo—fī
They may plow the ground.	hōo—fou
	wē—fou
	we found the cow.

Word Drill:

found	bow	round	mouth
house	how	sound	ground
mouse	plow	shout	frown
pound	loud	brown	south
wound	town	crowd	coward
count	towel	power	doubt
sour	cow	down	bound

1. I found a five leaf clover this morning.
2. We are looking for a small house all on one floor.
3. A mouse has gnawed a hole in the bag of grain.
4. She hurt her thumb when she tried to pound a nail in the wall.

5. I wound my eight-day clock yesterday.
6. Will you count these pennies for me?
7. Don't you find these grapefruit awfully sour?
8. He gave me a courteous bow as I passed him on the street.
9. How will you have your eggs, boiled or fried?
10. I must stay at the office and plow through the work.
11. Have I turned the TV up too loud for you?
12. We are going to town this morning. Can we get anything for you?
13. Please get me a towel; I want to wipe up this spilled coffee.
14. We drove round and round the block looking for a place to park.
15. The sound of the waves on the beach lulled me to sleep.
16. Give a shout when you are ready to go and I will be right with you.
17. Her hair used to be brown; I didn't recognize her as a blond.
18. There was such a crowd at the station I was afraid I would lose my bag.
19. We leave for Canada tonight. We are bound for Quebec.
20. The little village lies at the mouth of the river.
21. I have ground the pecans for the pie.
22. Wipe the frown off your face and try to look cheerful.
23. In the south people speak with a drawl.
24. I am really a coward when it comes to driving on icy roads.
25. I doubt that I will be able to go to the game on Saturday.
26. He said he would bow to my wishes and sell the property.
27. I found a mouse in the apple barrel.
28. They will soon plow the field for winter wheat.
29. His voice was so loud, I could see his wife frown at him.
30. She came from a small town in the south.
31. Will you pound the post into the ground for me?
32. The house she bought is an old brownstone.
33. Sound your horn so they will know we are waiting.
34. The snake wound itself around an old log.
35. I must count the stitches. I think I have dropped one.
36. Many people are very fond of sour pickles.

Lesson 9

37. The plow cut through the earth making straight furrows.
38. I must bow to your wishes.
39. Please keep your voice down and don't shout.
40. The child was as quiet as a mouse and never said a word.
41. We will have brown bread with the beans.
42. I think I have been around to every shop in town.
43. He frowned when I asked him to practice more.
44. Did you doubt his story?
45. We planted the spring bulbs on the south side of the house.
46. Have you ever milked a cow?
47. It is very hot down South.
48. My husband has just bought a new power mower.

LESSON 10

The Shape of the Sound of Long ī

ī—as in five and my

The sound of long ī is made up of the shape of the sound of ah, relaxed and open, followed rapidly by the sound of long ē, the lips draw slightly back and the opening of the lips narrows.

i

ie, igh, y, uy

Syllables:

why—mī—fī—shī—bī—thī—gī—sī—pī

Syllable Drill:

Ī—mō	hōō—mou—sī	thā—sā—whī
thā—mō	hōō—mā—fī	thā—sā—mī
mō—pī	thā—mā—fī	hōō—sā—mī
mā—pī	thā—mā—bī	hōō—plā—fī
mā—Ī	bī—ā—hou	wē—plā—fī
bā—pī	They may buy a house.	hē—plā—fī
May I bake a pie?		He plays the fife.

Word Drill:

guide	buy	sight
fife	my	shine
find	scythe	ripe
five	shy	time
pie	sign	kind
size	why	while
sigh	mile	wire
wife	fine	like
by	wipe	white

Lesson 10

1. My son is blind and has a seeing eye guide dog.
2. My brother plays the fife in a fife and drum corps.
3. Do you think you can find a house you like?
4. It has been five years since I last saw my sister.
5. Which kind of pie do you prefer: apple, pecan or lemon?
6. The blouse the shop sent me is the wrong size.
7. She gave a sigh of relief when the lesson was over.
8. Jack's wife is a very good cook.
9. I always come to work by the turnpike.
10. He said he would buy my painting for fifty dollars.
11. That is the least of my worries.
12. Father Time is always shown holding a scythe.
13. She is very shy and does not like to meet strangers.
14. Didn't you see the sign "No Smoking?"
15. Why didn't you let me know you couldn't come yesterday?
16. It is just a mile from my house to the beach.
17. Her hair is so fine she has trouble arranging it.
18. If you wash the dishes, I'll wipe them for you.
19. I caught sight of Jean and Arthur at the ball game.
20. Dicky works as a shoe shine boy on Saturdays.
21. The time is ripe for a change of policy.
22. Will you tell me the time please?
23. What kind of shows do you like to watch on TV?
24. I had the house painted while I was away. Do you like the color?
25. I sent a wire to my brother asking him to come for Christmas.
26. We like to take a long walk on Sundays, usually to the dike.
27. White upholstery gets soiled very quickly.
28. The rhubarb is ripe. Let's make a pie.
29. I can't find my keys; maybe I dropped them.
30. The doctor says John is losing his sight.
31. We drove miles through the desert. It was very tiresome.
32. What size notebook do you want me to get you?
33. If only the sun would shine; we have had enough rain.
34. Five people came to my house today trying to sell something.
35. Why do you sigh so much? Are you unhappy?
36. These pears look fine and ripe.

37. The little girl was very shy and wouldn't speak.
38. I went by your house. I like the color you painted your front door.
39. They say there are many wires down after the storm.
40. Have you ever tried to use a scythe?
41. While you are in town, will you pick up an apple pie for me?
42. He is very kind and offered me a job in his office.
43. I had to pay a two dollar fine for parking too long.
44. Her face was white from shock and fright.
45. I must wipe off the venetian blinds today.
46. One of my girls plays the fife, the other the piano.
47. My time is completely taken. I will let you know as soon as I am free.
48. I think I'll buy some sheets at the white sale.

LESSON 11

The Shape of the Sound of
oi—oy

oi—oy—as in oil and boy

The sound of oi is also made up of two sounds. The sound of aw with the lips slightly puckered and the opening rather round, followed rapidly by the sound of long ē, the lips drawing back slightly at the corners and the lip opening narrow.

oi—oy

Syllables:

moi—shoi—voi—boy—soi—poi—foi

Syllable Drill:

fah—fou	mā—fou	whī—fou
fah—mō	mā—soi	thā—fou
wē—mō	hōō—soi	fou—shoi
wē—soi	hōō—moi	fou—coi
thā—soi	hōō—shoi	Ī—fou
thā—voi	hōō—boy	fou—coi
hē—voi	Who is my boy?	I found a coin.
He hears my voice.		

Word Drill:

hoist	toil	loyal
boil	moist	toy
soil	join	royal
voice	noise	loiter
boy	coin	joy
foil	broil	doily
roil	coil	foist

Compare:

Shall I	Will I	I shall	I will
Shall we	Will we	We shall	We will
Shall they	Will they	They shall	They will

1. The janitor will hoist the flag at the school.
2. I have put the water on to boil. We will have tea in a minute.
3. The soil is not rich enough. You should put on some fertilizer.
4. He has a beautiful tenor voice and sings in the choir.
5. I must pay the paper boy what I owe him today.
6. What would we do these days without aluminum foil?
7. If you roil the water, the fish won't bite.
8. Shoveling snow is toil that is dangerous.
9. The atmosphere is so moist, I can't get anything to dry.
10. Will you join us this afternoon? We're going to the movies.
11. The noise of the traffic kept me awake all night.
12. A coin machine is called a one-armed bandit.
13. Few women wear their hair in a coil around their head anymore.
14. I thought I was going to broil, sitting in the sun watching the game.
15. She is a very kind and loyal friend.
16. I must buy a toy for my niece's baby.
17. The prince wore a royal purple velvet cape.
18. Boys who loiter on the corner in the evening are usually up to no good.
19. Their joy at seeing each other after so long was very touching.
20. Will you make me a doily set to use as place mats?
21. Don't think you can foist that job off on me.
22. Shall I broil the fish for dinner?
23. They will join us later when they have finished their business.
24. We will flip a coin to see who must rake the leaves.
25. I shall voice an opinion on the matter if asked.
26. We should hard boil some eggs for the picnic.
27. Don't loiter in the playground after school; come straight home.
28. Shall we go to the toy shop and do some Christmas shopping?

Lesson 11

29. Will you help me to hoist this bag onto the rack?
30. John and I went to school together when we were boys.
31. You must always be loyal to your country.
32. A three leaf clover is called a trefoil.
33. Did you soil your trousers while changing the tire?
34. Have you the right coins to make a call from a public phone?
35. The noise in the subway is unbearable.
36. She is a good cook and her cake was nice and moist.
37. I am going to join my sister for a trip through Spain.
38. Please coil the hose and put it in the garage for the winter.
39. Many buildings have a sign in the entry saying "no loitering allowed."
40. I have a bad cold and have lost my voice.
41. I don't like to broil food as it soils the oven.
42. We toiled all Saturday spading the flower beds.
43. The poor man has a painful boil on his neck.
44. I hope you will join our bridge club.
45. My little grandson is a great joy to me. He is always so jolly.
46. I will put a doily under that vase so it won't scratch the table.
47. Please don't toy with the window shade; you will break the spring.
48. The lesson is over. You may join your friends.

LESSON 12

The Shape of the Sound of k and Hard c

k—as in keep
hard c—as in cold

The k and hard c are the same as hard g. They have no visible shape; k and hard c are deeper in the throat than hard g. The air is expelled when the sound is made. In some people a slight movement of the neck muscles may be visible. This sound must usually be realized by the context.

k and hard c

Syllables:

    kĭ—cā—cōō—kē—cō—cou—coi—cŏŏ

Syllable Drill:

hē—mā	fah—sō—cā	hōō—sō—coi
hē—sā	fah—mō—kī	hōō—sō—kē
hē—sō	thā—mō—kī	thē—sā—kē
shē—sō	thā—fō—cŏŏ	thē—dā—kē
sō—cōō	shē—fō—cŏŏ	thē—dā—cōō
sō—kī	shē—fĭ—cŏŏ	The day is so cool.
She is so kind.	She is a fine cook.	

Word Drill:

car	cape	pick
calf	case	leak
call	cave	walk
cargo	count	bank
can	cow	think
card	coil	sank
coal	come	wink
cold	cup	tank
coat	cook	link

Lesson 12

cool	cut	pink
coop	keep	caught
cake	key	cover
came	kind	talk

1. Have you been driving a car many years?
2. A calf is very ungainly when it first tries to walk.
3. I put in a long distance call to California.
4. The ship left with a cargo of ammunition for our troops.
5. I can meet you tomorrow at the club.
6. I have lost the card bearing my social security number.
7. There are many coal mines in West Virginia.
8. A salad should be cold and crisp.
9. I need a new winter coat; I have worn this one for at least five years.
10. It is good to feel the cool breeze this evening; today was so hot.
11. I have never tried to bake a cake. I'm not much of a cook.
12. We have a chicken coop in our back yard.
13. My brother and sister-in-law came down to spend Christmas with me.
14. I never find a cape very comfortable to wear. I like to have my arms free.
15. In case I can't go with you, I will call.
16. The children love to play in the cave; it excites their imagination.
17. I know I can count on her help with the work.
18. I was once chased by a mad cow and I am afraid of them.
19. I left a coil of picture wire on the mantel. Will you get it for me?
20. Will you come with me while I change my book at the library?
21. The recipe calls for a cup of sugar and two eggs.
22. My sister will cook the Thanksgiving dinner this year.
23. I cut my finger on a piece of paper and it is very sore.
24. We had to keep the children indoors all day, it rained so hard.

25. Have you an extra front door key you could lend me?
26. They are such kind neighbors, always ready to help in an emergency.
27. I always get my arms scratched when I pick raspberries.
28. There is a bad leak in the bathroom and I am afraid the ceiling will fall.
29. I try to take a long walk every weekend.
30. I met Tom in the bank and we had quite a chat.
31. Do you think it wise to let the children take the car tonight?
32. They told me the boat sank a few miles off shore.
33. I didn't get a wink of sleep last night; my boy was sick.
34. The tank of the hot water heater has sprung a leak.
35. Pink is not my favorite color.
36. A chain is as strong as its weakest link.
37. I caught my heel in a crack in the sidewalk and twisted my ankle.
38. I'll just put the cover over my typewriter and we'll go.
39. My lawyer will talk to the owner of the property for me.
40. The truck that overturned was carrying a cargo of chickens.
41. Keep your cool. We will be out of this mess soon.
42. I have lost the key to my briefcase.
43. Please put more charcoal in the grill.
44. I called the bank and asked them to mail me my statement.
45. I was so hot from walking, I had to take off my coat and carry it.
46. I hope I can count on you not to let the news leak out.
47. She is going to pick me up in her car.
48. I think you have done very well with this lesson.

LESSON 13

The Shape of the Sound of Short ă

ă—as in map

Short ă has the widest opening of the lips for short vowels, the corners of the lips slightly drawn back and a slight drop of the jaw.

Short ă

Syllables:

thă—shă—mă—fă—bă—kă—vă—să—gă

Syllable Drill:

hōō căn gō	how fah ăm
hōō căn sē	how fah ră
thā căn sē	hōō fah ră
thā căn mă	hōō ră fă
hē căn mă	hē ră fă
hē căn că	He ran fast.
He can catch the man.	

Word Drill:

ban	path	stamp
plan	fast	catch
than	ran	value
man	sap	bad
fan	band	pan
land	pass	sand
lamp	latch	bat
hand	match	map
pack	cash	can
thank	rang	cab

1. Every nation should ban the use of the atom bomb.
2. We plan to open our hat shop next month.
3. It's later than I thought; we must go home.
4. I'm looking for a man to do gardening for me.
5. This electric fan needs to be oiled.
6. How much land goes with your house?
7. Please sit over there. You will find that lamp gives better light.
8. I make my child hold my hand when crossing the street.
9. Would you mind if I stopped at the drugstore for a pack of cigarettes.
10. She came to thank me for the coffee cake I made for her.
11. This path goes through the woods to the cove.
12. You speak too fast for me to be able to lipread you.
13. The boy ran out from behind a car and was knocked down.
14. This weather will make the sap run in the trees.
15. I used to play the fife in our school band.
16. Don't pass the car ahead on the right.
17. Will you latch the door for me? My hands are full as you see.
18. Have you a match? I left my lighter at home.
19. The supermarket refused to cash the check for me.
20. I rang your doorbell yesterday but no one answered.
21. I must get an airmail stamp for this letter.
22. If you don't hurry, you won't catch the bus.
23. Please tell me what value you would place on this old coin.
24. There has been a very bad fire in the shopping district.
25. Will you see if you can match this thread for me while you are out?
26. Should you pass a newsstand, please pick up a paper for me.
27. Does this hot humid weather sap your energy?
28. You should see the stacks of fan mail some singers get.
29. My hands were so cold I couldn't unlatch the door.
30. I must pack a bag for my trip tomorrow.
31. If you keep your wet shoes on, you may catch cold.
32. Thank you for your nice long letter.

Lesson 13

33. They are trying to ban the sales of cigarettes in hospitals.
34. The light from this lamp isn't strong enough for sewing.
35. He is inclined to follow the path of least resistance.
36. Just hand me my work basket, will you please?
37. I rang up to see if you would care to come over for supper.
38. If you put an elastic band around those papers, you won't drop any.
39. The plane is supposed to land at eight-thirty.
40. When do they plan to open the new school?
41. The boy ran away so fast we couldn't catch up with him.
42. I value his opinion very highly.
43. The pan is very hot; don't burn yourself.
44. Will you wait while I take the sand out of my shoes?
45. Bats fly at night. They can't see in the daylight.
46. I am afraid we are lost. Let me look at the road map.
47. Can you go with me tomorrow?
48. I will phone for a cab to take you to the station.

LESSON 14

The Shape of the Sound of Short ĭ—y

ĭ—y as in sit and pity

Short ĭ and y show a small relaxed lip opening; the sound also has a slight drawing back of the corners of the mouth.

Short ĭ—y

Syllables:

mĭ–fĭ–kĭ–wĭ–bĭ–shĭ–whĭ–gĭ–thĭ–pĭ

Syllable Drill:

whī–wĭ	hoō dĭ sē
thā–wĭ	thā dĭ sē
hoō–wĭ	yoō dĭ sē
wĭ pā	dĭ sē mĭ
Ī wĭ	dĭ sē wĭ
pā bĭ	dĭ sē fĭ
I will pay the bill.	Did you see the fish?

Word Drill:

thin	rim	rich
minute	kill	mint
will	sift	list
win	ship	mid
bin	thick	pick
pin	live	silk
sin	chip	did
finish	slip	sick
bill	fish	rid
film	miss	tip

1. I wish I could lose weight and be as thin as Mary.
2. Have you a minute to spare? I would like to show you this book.

Lesson 14

3. I will go with you to town at two o'clock.
4. Did you ever win anything in a raffle?
5. I must see if I still have potatoes in my vegetable bin.
6. What a beautiful emerald pin! Did your husband give it to you?
7. Some people consider it a sin to overeat.
8. When do you think you will finish writing your book?
9. Please send my bill for the dresses to this address.
10. I must pick up more film for my camera.
11. How did you break the rim of your glasses?
12. My bout of flu was so severe I thought it would kill me.
13. They are trying to sift the evidence but have no real clues.
14. On what ship are you sailing for Europe?
15. The fog was so thick I could only see a few feet ahead.
16. Do you live in town or in the suburbs?
17. Try not to chip the cups when you are washing them.
18. Will you slip this letter in the mailbox when you go out?
19. Were the fish biting or have you come home empty handed?
20. If the taxi doesn't come soon, I will miss my train.
21. Her uncle is quite rich. He is head of a large firm.
22. Have you tried drinking mint tea to make you sleep?
23. I have mislaid my shopping list as usual.
24. I always have a hungry feeling in midafternoon.
25. In his will he left his whole estate to charity.
26. You will have to thin the paint or you will make a mess of the job.
27. The minute I felt a bite, I reeled in my hook.
28. There is a thick film of oil on the water from the motor boats.
29. I hope you will miss me while I am away.
30. The robin had a large worm hanging from his bill.
31. He has already made a mint of money from his new venture.
32. Will you sift these ingredients together while I break the eggs?
33. Live and let live is my motto.
34. Little Jackie is certainly a chip off the old block.
35. Be careful, don't slip on the wet floor.
36. They are both fond of food with rich sauces.

37. He never goes hunting because he hates to kill anything.
38. I wish I had a thick juicy rare steak this minute.
39. I think the accident occurred in midmorning.
40. Would you try to pin this corsage on for me?
41. If I win the sweepstake, I will go to South America.
42. You can give me the guest list; I'll send out the invitations.
43. Please pick some string beans for me from the garden.
44. She wore a yellow silk blouse.
45. Where did you go on your camping trip?
46. My husband was sick so we couldn't go to the dinner.
47. I think I will never get rid of this cold.
48. John gave the waiter a generous tip.

LESSON 15

The Shape of the Sound of Short ŭ and h Before a Vowel

ŭ—as in but or fun
  Short ŭ has a medium opening of the lips and a definite drop of the jaw.

h—before a vowel as in ham and hope
  This sound has no movement, but the mouth is wide open as the word begins. The breath is expelled causing a prolonged movement of the vowel which follows it.

Short ŭ and h (before a vowel)

Syllables:
  shŭ—rŭ—bŭ—thŭ—fŭ—sŭ—gŭ
  hŭ—hĭ—hă—hō—hī—hē—hah—how—hoi—hā

Syllable Drill:

how gā	wĭ gō hŭ
hoō gā	wĭ gō bŭ
hoō grē	mā gō shŭ
shē—grē	shă gō shŭ
shē-hă	shă gō lŭ
grē thŭ	Shall we go to lunch?
She has a green thumb.	

Word Drill:

bump	tough	hoop
fun	drum	haven
sum	crust	harp
lump	lunch	has
rough	touch	hump
trust	hope	heat
punch	head	his
brush	hut	held
dull	high	hot
thumb	halt	him

1. The way that man is driving, I'm afraid he will bump into us.
2. Did you have fun on the winter cruise?
3. Now let us sum up what has been said.
4. The boy has a lump on his forehead. He fell off his bike.
5. My hands are very rough from the cold weather.
6. Will you trust me to look after little Bobby this afternoon?
7. The conductor hasn't come through the train yet to punch our tickets.
8. I must stop at the drugstore for a toothbrush.
9. The after-dinner speeches were all so dull last evening.
10. She caught her thumb in the car door and has lost her nail.
11. I told the butcher that the meat he sold me last week was very tough.
12. My son wanted a drum for his birthday.
13. Do you make your own pie crust or buy it frozen?
14. Lunch will be at 12:30 and the meeting will follow it.
15. Do you use the touch system on the typewriter, or hunt and peck?
16. They will find the lost child, I hope.
17. My head aches from the noise and confusion.
18. The children built a little hut in the woods.
19. How high is the wall around your property?
20. They are trying desperately to halt the epidemic.
21. I really need a larger embroidery hoop.
22. She is in the hospital in New Haven.
23. A woman can look very graceful playing the harp.
24. His son has just graduated from college.
25. Their new business is doing better. I think they are over the hump.
26. Would you please turn down the heat? The room is awfully warm.
27. He is a stranger. I don't think he knows his way around town.
28. The dinner was held at the new restaurant called The Hut.
29. One should eat a hot meal at least once a day.
30. My son left for California. I miss him very much.
31. The country roads around here are very rough.
32. A group of teenagers had a brush with the police last night.

33. Children think it's fun to roll a hoop.
34. I didn't think the show had much punch; I was disappointed.
35. My cold makes my head feel so dull and hot.
36. There is a crust on the snow after the freezing rain.
37. They served champagne punch at the reception.
38. Have you ever tried to thumb a ride?
39. I held a lump of sugar out to the horse.
40. The small boat reached haven before the rough sea capsized it.
41. My boy is not good at sums. He thinks only of playing the drum.
42. I trust the headmaster of the school. He is doing a fine job.
43. The heat and humidity are so high today, it's very trying.
44. I threw a crust of bread to the squirrel.
45. I bumped into Grace while out for lunch.
46. I have lost touch with him these last few years.
47. They called a halt to the games because it was so hot.
48. Did the accident cause the lump on your head?

LESSON 16

The Shape of the Sound of Short ĕ and l

ĕ—as in bell
   Short ĕ has a medium lip opening and a very definite dropping of the lower lip and jaw.

l—as in lamp
   In the sound of l, the tip of the tongue touches the palate just back of the upper teeth and descends against the back of the upper teeth. The movement is seen as the tongue descends.

Short ĕ and l

Syllables:
   bĕ—gĕ—fĕ—hĕ—mĕ—thĕ—pĕ—whĕ—lĕ
   lā—lah—lō—lōō—lī—lou—lē—loi—lĭ—law—lă

Syllable Drill:

thā că sĕ	mā wē sī mă
hōō că sĕ	mā wē fī mă
hōō că fĕ	mā wē lī thŭ
shē wĭ fĕ	mā wē lī lă
hē wĭ fĕ	May we light the lamp?
hē wĭ mĕ	
He will mend my fence.	

Word Drill:

mend	sell	lift
bell	ready	large
fell	west	lump
well	shelf	self
rest	chest	look
met	rent	lose
led	sense	whole
melt	letter	while
tell	leave	feel
felt	lamp	boil

Lesson 16

1. I will mend those socks for you.
2. Didn't you hear the doorbell ringing?
3. The window cleaner fell from the second story window.
4. I don't think she is well. She always complains of feeling tired.
5. Can you go the rest of the way alone?
6. I met her brother last year in Florida.
7. I led the children in singing Christmas carols.
8. If it stays so cold, the snow will never melt.
9. Won't you tell us about your trip to India?
10. I have not felt at all well this week; perhaps I am getting the flu.
11. My husband wants to sell the house in the spring.
12. Will you be ready to go with me to town at two o'clock?
13. The whole family went out West to a ranch.
14. I have a bad cold; it has gone down on my chest.
15. Please dust the books on the bottom shelf for me.
16. If the rent goes up again, we will have to move.
17. The story she told didn't make sense to me.
18. I haven't had a letter from Sue in weeks and I am worried about her.
19. Is it tomorrow you leave on your trip?
20. I need a new lamp for my living room.
21. Would you lift the suitcase up onto the rack for me please?
22. The house my sister bought is large and rambling.
23. I don't think you can lift that heavy box by yourself.
24. How much sugar do you like in your coffee, one lump or two?
25. I would love to look at the pictures you took at the party.
26. If you go for a walk in the woods, be careful not to lose your way.
27. The whole family sent their love to you.
28. While I was out shopping, I lost one of my gloves.
29. Do you feel well enough to go with us?
30. It's time I put the potatoes to boil if we are to have dinner at seven.
31. Don't try to lift that chest. You will strain your back.
32. The recipe calls for a large lump of butter.

33. I fell off the ladder when trying to reach the top shelf.
34. Do have a little sense. You know you are trying to do too much.
35. I took my watch to be repaired. They said it would be ready Tuesday.
36. I broke one of her best cups and I felt miserable.
37. What else can we put on this shelf?
38. There is a nice cool west wind blowing.
39. Please tell me if you feel a draft from that window.
40. You shouldn't let the children leave their toys on the floor.
41. The candle has melted and dropped wax on the tablecloth.
42. I am going to look for some felt to make the skirt of my costume.
43. I can't hear the telephone bell when it rings.
44. One thing led to another and we decided to rent a house on the west side.
45. The automat is a self-service restaurant.
46. He says the rest will make me feel stronger.
47. Will you wait a moment while I look for my keys?
48. We are going to sell our house and rent an apartment.

LESSON 17

The Shape of the Sound of Short ŏ and ch

ŏ—as in chop or pond
Some teachers of lipreading omit the short ŏ because so often it is pronounced either like ah, as in rock or as aw in dog. However, when pronounced as a true short ŏ, there is a quick forward movement of the lips with medium opening.

ch—as in cheese
The lips are thrust forward and have a rather square shape.

Short ŏ and ch
as in chop

Syllables:

    pŏp–tŏp–sŏp–mŏp–lŏp–ŏn–ŏp–ŏk
    chă–chī–chē–chā–chō–chōō–chŏ–chah

Syllable Drill:

Hōō wĭ pŏp	Ī shă chōō
Hōō wĭ lŏp	You că chōō
Thē chī lŏp	Chōō thē chŏ
Thē chī hŏp	Shē wĭ chōō
chī lī hŏp	She will choose the chop.
The child likes to hop.	

Word Drill:

mop	clock	shock
top	rock	hop
Bob	flock	shop
pop	sock	church
knob	knock	chimes
drop	cock	chapel
chop	dock	choose
Robert	slot	choice

pond	knot	cheese
frog	stop	china
lock	hot	chosen

1. Please mop the bedroom floor.
2. The papers are in the top drawer.
3. The car belongs to my brother Bob.
4. Let's pop some corn this evening.
5. The door knob is very stiff and needs oil.
6. Did you drop these keys?
7. I would like a broiled lamb chop for dinner.
8. Robert is a very smart young lawyer.
9. We have water lilies in our pond at home.
10. A frog has very bulging eyes.
11. I must have the lock on the back door changed.
12. I will meet you at twelve o'clock for lunch.
13. I stubbed my toe on a rock in the road.
14. We saw a flock of birds flying south.
15. Give me your sock and I will mend the hole.
16. Please knock before entering the room.
17. The cock wakes me up every morning with his crowing.
18. The ship is due to dock at eleven o'clock.
19. Put a dime in the slot and you will get a stamp.
20. I can't undo the knot in my shoe lace.
21. Will you stop at the pharmacy and pick up my prescription?
22. We have had a very hot summer and I am glad that fall is here.
23. The news of Dave's death was a great shock to us.
24. Children like to hop and skip instead of walking.
25. I went to the new shop to look at the dresses.
26. If you are looking for the church, it is just around the corner.
27. I love to hear the chimes striking the hour.
28. The school has a beautiful chapel.
29. Which suit will you choose, the grey or the brown?
30. The choice of restaurant is up to you.
31. I am very fond of all kinds of cheese, but Swiss is my favorite.
32. She received some very fine china as a wedding present.

Lesson 17

33. Robert was chosen to head the committee.
34. Please drop what you are doing and come with me to the shop.
35. I asked Bob to chop some wood for the stove.
36. Be careful not to rock the boat as you get in.
37. Will you turn the door knob for me as my hands are full?
38. We have not had a drop of rain for two months.
39. There is a choice of cheeses on the top shelf.
40. Did you see the frog hop into the pond?
41. It is so hot, I can't mop and dust this morning.
42. Can you see the clock on the church steeple?
43. Do you know how to tie a Turk's head knot?
44. I bought my little nephew a pop gun.
45. I have never seen a cock fight, have you?
46. There are several good shops in town from which to choose.
47. My new china tea cups have a floral pattern.
48. Be sure to lock your car when you park it.

LESSON 18

The Shape of the Vowel Sound of er—ir—ur

er—ir—ur—as in her—bird—fur

These all look alike. There is a forward movement of the lips, the movement being particularly noticeable in the lower lip.

Vowel sound of
er—ir—ur

Syllables:

bur—fur—sir—pur—thir—shir—wer—ter—ler

Syllable Drill:

thā bur	how law
how bur	thā law
how thir	thā gir
hē thir	thē gir
hē kir	gir law
wĭ ler	law pur
ler lĕs	The girl lost her purse.
He will learn his lesson.	

Word Drill:

fur	worm	ferns
first	work	hurt
surf	purr	pearl
serve	purse	verb
were	girl	nerve
her	third	turn
firm	shirk	learn
verse	word	burn
curve	chirp	heard
bird	perch	stern
worth	worse	search

Lesson 18

1. We must serve dinner right away.
2. The rolls were nice and crisp.
3. Her maiden name was Brown.
4. Can you recite some verse for us?
5. Is this the first time you have visited Mt. Vernon?
6. The man has a very firm hand shake.
7. Are you an enthusiastic bird watcher?
8. The girl at the counter will take your order.
9. It is too warm to wear a fur coat.
10. Do you enjoy surf bathing?
11. Be careful. This road has a very dangerous curve.
12. My kitten always purrs when I hold her on my lap.
13. The canary was sitting on his perch singing.
14. You usually find ferns in the woods.
15. Bill gave Jane a pearl necklace on their tenth wedding anniversary.
16. You should use the past tense of the verb.
17. We will go on our vacation the third week of July.
18. Please don't shirk your practicing.
19. The birds chirp outside my window early in the morning.
20. The first time I went to London it rained all the time I was there.
21. I am afraid I left my purse at home.
22. Were you hurt when the limb fell from the tree?
23. My brother loves surfing.
24. The stairs were built with a very graceful curve.
25. The paddle steamer churned its way down the river.
26. Have you heard the rumor that is going around?
27. Her father is a stockbroker.
28. The song had many verses.
29. The firm is well-known for its honesty.
30. He wormed his way into my confidence.
31. The work will take me at least a week.
32. No word has reached us of their arrival.
33. After the next traffic light, you should turn right.
34. Did you learn to speak Spanish when you were a child?

35. There is no wind today so we can burn the leaves.
36. Have you heard the evening news on TV?
37. I injured a nerve in my elbow when I fell.
38. Will you serve wine with the dinner?
39. I could hear the purr of the engine in the dark.
40. The boys will hurt each other if they play so roughly.
41. You are the first to criticize the report.
42. It's my firm belief that you will get the job if you try.
43. Mary's girl is a friend of my daughter's.
44. The third house from the corner is where I live.
45. I feel that my husband is not stern enough with the children.
46. I have just dropped my key. Will you help me search for it?
47. We had even a worse storm last year at this time.
48. Please tell me how the word is spelled.

LESSON 19

The Shape of the Sound of r Before and After a Vowel

r—as in rain or rose

There is a forward movement of the lips, particularly the bottom lip, and the tip of the tongue turns upward toward the palate.

r before and after a vowel

Syllables:

rā—rī—raw—rōō—rē—rah—rō—roi

Syllable Drill:

Shē fah	Hōō ah rā
Thā fah	Hōō ah raw
Hōō fah	thā ah rō
Hōō cah	pā ah rō
my cah	pā ah rī
cah rĕ	The pears are ripe.
My car is red.	

Word Drill:

read	ripe	wear	core
rest	raise	wore	share
rich	road	pour	car
rough	rain	hour	four
raw	rust	sour	bear
raft	rose	far	sure
room	real	here	fair (fare)
rush	row	are	fire
rock	Roy	more	roar
rope	soar	pear	seashore

1. Will you read her letter to me?
2. My head aches. I think I will lie down and rest.
3. Everyone wishes they had a rich uncle.
4. Do your hands get rough and chapped in winter?

5. There is a very raw wind blowing today.
6. The boys swam out to the raft to practice diving.
7. I don't have room in my suitcase for these shoes.
8. I usually get up early so that I won't have to rush.
9. Let's sit on this flat rock and wait for the others to catch up.
10. I'll throw you the rope. Make the boat fast.
11. The strawberries won't be ripe for another week.
12. I was so sick I couldn't raise my head from the pillow.
13. I don't think we have driven over this road before.
14. Take your umbrella. I think it's going to rain.
15. Better to wear out than rust out.
16. I picked this rose a short while ago. There is still dew on it.
17. Those artificial flowers look almost real.
18. What row are our seats in? Not too far back, I hope.
19. Roy is my neighbor's son; he's a nice lad.
20. I think I will wear my new dress to the party tonight.
21. The cost of living continues to soar.
22. The children wore snow jackets to school.
23. Will you pour the coffee while I cut us some cake?
24. Do you find these grapefruit awfully sour?
25. How far is the station from your house?
26. They will be here in a quarter of an hour. They just telephoned.
27. What are your plans for the summer, will your children be with you?
28. We could do a better job if we had more time.
29. Would you like a pear for dessert, or would you rather have cake?
30. Throw your apple core in the pail.
31. Will you share a taxi with me?
32. My car broke down this morning and I was late for work.
33. They gave us four seats for the show.
34. I can't bear to think that vacation is over tomorrow.
35. Are you sure you are comfortable in that chair?
36. The paper says the weather will be fair tomorrow.

Lesson 19

37. There was a big fire two blocks from where we live.
38. I could hear the roar of the engine before the car came in sight.
39. At the seashore we take our lunch to the beach every day.
40. How much is the fare on the bus?
41. It rests me to lie down and read.
42. I am not at all sure that we are on the right road.
43. The water was very rough. It made it hard to row to shore.
44. She wore a corsage of roses at the dinner.
45. If you rush, you may just catch your bus.
46. The road was very rough and there were many rocks in it.
47. Roy's father is far from being rich, but they are comfortable.
48. Here is your next lesson to practice.

LESSON 20

The Shape of the Sound of n Before and After a Vowel

n—as in name or noise

The flat edge of the tongue touches the palate. Although the lips are parted, the upper and lower teeth are quite close together making it difficult to see the tongue movement.

n before and after a vowel

Syllables:

nah—now—nī—nō—naw—noō—nā—noi—nur—nă—nĭ—nŭ—ně

Syllable Drill:

Plē mā sē	Thā că now
Plē bō sē	Thā că nah
Plē sō noō	că noō nah
Plē thē noō	hă noō nah
Plē thrĕ noō	hă noō nŭ
Plē thrĕ nē	I have a new number.
Please thread my needle.	

Word Drill:

name	knee	on	pen
know	nuts	gone	than
knew	nurse	in	when
now	nine	been	pin
nothing	number	seen	win
noise	noon	can	sun
night	needle	man	done
nephew	nice	ran	none
knife	gnawed	fun	ton
newspaper	annoys	main	gun

Lesson 20

1. What name did they give their new baby?
2. Do you know what time your father's train arrives?
3. I like some homemade chocolate cake now and then.
4. I tried to match this silk but they had nothing like it.
5. Please don't make a noise; you will wake the baby.
6. The night before last we had a bad thunder storm.
7. My nephew's job takes him to Europe twice a year.
8. Will you lend me your pen knife to cut this cord?
9. The afternoon newspaper carried the whole story.
10. I missed the step and twisted my knee.
11. Will you chop the nuts for the pecan pie?
12. The nurse said that the patient is much better this morning.
13. He had nine grandchildren.
14. Give me your telephone number and I will call you.
15. It is nearly noon. We had better decide where to lunch.
16. I have dropped my knitting needle somewhere and can't find it.
17. Wasn't it nice that your boss gave you the day off?
18. The mouse gnawed a hole in the bag of meal.
19. It annoys me when the telephone stops ringing before I can answer.
20. I am going on a cruise in June.
21. My cousin has gone to the Netherlands.
22. I will be in tomorrow if you can come then.
23. We have been touring Europe all summer.
24. We have not seen our friends the Browns for three months.
25. Can you bake bread?
26. The man I engaged for the job will be here at noon.
27. When I heard the fire engine, I ran to see where it was stopping.
28. We had such fun at our class reunion.
29. The main thing is to drive carefully.
30. I think my pen needs a refill; it has run dry.
31. The job was more than I bargained for.
32. When will you call the next meeting of the committee?

33. Did you ever play "Pin the Tail on the Donkey?"
34. Who do you think will win the election?
35. The hot sun will soon dry the washing I hung out.
36. I don't know what I have done with my keys.
37. I knew I would miss my appointment; the train was so late.
38. I asked Nelson to get me a notebook, but he found they had none.
39. The stone I was trying to move felt as though it weighed a ton.
40. Do you believe we should have stricter gun laws?
41. Do you know the name of the new school principal?
42. I need nothing at the store but a package of needles.
43. Did you see the story in the newspaper of the nine car accident?
44. The nurse took the patient's temperature at night.
45. My knee pains me more than ever.
46. The main thing is to cut down the noise.
47. Now what number did you ask for, nine or ninety?
48. At noon when I am out I will take the knife to be sharpened.

LESSON 21

The Shape of the Sound of
y as in You and Words Ending in yer, ior

y—as in you and lawyer or senior

The lips have a narrow relaxed opening followed by a dropping of the jaw. The shape of this sound is difficult to see as it starts with an expulsion of breath in the back of the throat; sometimes a movement may be seen in the muscles of the throat just under the jaw bone.

y as in you and words ending in yer, ior

Syllables:

yah–yō–yōō–yē–yaw–yă–yĕ–yĭ–yŏ–yŭ–yer

Syllable Drill:

mī yah	hōō yer
mī yō	hōō yaw
mī yaw	thē yaw
mī yōō	thē yē
yōō mā	thē yă
yōō mā yē	thē yōō
You may yield your power.	The Yankee youth yearned for a yawl.

Word Drill:

you	yonder	yarn
your	Yule	yawl
yard	yip	yield
young	yearn	lawyer
youth	yeast	employer
yet	yellow	destroyer
yawn	yesterday	senior
yoke	Yankee	junior
year	yacht	
yodel	yank	

63

1. Will you tell me if you can't hear me?
2. The apple tree yonder is about a hundred years old.
3. I cleaned up the yard on Saturday.
4. I think the girl is too young to be dating.

5. I haven't been able to reach him by phone.
6. The lecture was so long I began to yawn.
7. They got a yoke of oxen to pull the car out of the mud.
8. What year did you go to France?

9. Did you ever hear a Swiss mountaineer yodel?
10. The youth was much too sure of himself.
11. The Yule log is always lighted on Christmas eve.
12. Some small dogs yip constantly.

13. Everyone yearns for the war to be over quickly.
14. I shall need to buy some yeast if I am going to make bread.
15. The yellow sweater is very becoming to you.
16. Yesterday was our tenth wedding anniversary.

17. A foreigner thinks every American is a Yankee.
18. The old sailor told a very good yarn.
19. My brother has a thirty foot yawl and cruises all summer.
20. Our fruit trees didn't yield a very good crop this year.

21. You will need to engage a lawyer to fight the case for you.
22. A sailing yacht under full sail is a beautiful sight.
23. He tells me that his employer is a very considerate man.
24. Is Clarence the senior or junior partner of the firm?

25. The Japanese beetle is a great destroyer of flower gardens.
26. Don't yank so hard on the reins; you will hurt the horse's mouth.
27. Your new car is a beauty. How many miles have you driven it?
28. Will you buy me a yard and a half of ecru linen when you are out?

29. A young dog should be trained to obey.
30. I like the dress but I think it is a little too youthful for me.
31. I am not yet ready to retire and take it easy.
32. Sometimes I get eggs that have two yolks.

Lesson 21

33. I left there the year of the big hurricane.
34. If you yawn so hard you will dislocate your jaw.
35. Do you like the sweater made of heavy yarn?
36. The destroyer cut through the water on its way to sea.

37. Yank the bell cord and we will see if anyone is at home.
38. I yearn to have news of my brother who is ill.
39. I will yield to his wishes and sell the house.
40. We got our tickets for the trip yesterday.

41. My daughter is at college. She is a junior this year.
42. How good a case does your lawyer think you have?
43. I love my new yellow roadster.
44. The senior class is graduating tomorrow.

45. Leave it to youth to enjoy winter sports.
46. Year after year we go the same place for our holiday.
47. She is young and will be able to do the hard work.
48. Her employer gave her a raise last week.

LESSON 22

The Shape of the Sound of d and t

d—as in dime
t—as in team

The movement is the same as for n: the flat edge of the tongue touches the palate, the lips are parted, upper and lower teeth quite close together. However, the movement is more rapid than for n and as the tongue drops down to take the vowel, there is a more marked jaw movement.

d and t

Syllables:

dā—doō—dī—dō—der—dou—dē—daw—dĕ—dĭ—dă
tā—toō—tī—tō—ter—tou—tē—tă—tĭ—tŭ—tĕ

Syllable Drill:

fah toō gā	sē fah
mā toō gā	gō fah
mā toi loō	toō fah
ou toi loō	fah dō
ou tah wĭ	dō gō
ou tē wŭ	yoō gō
Our team won.	Don't you go too far.

Word Drill:

team	time	dime
debt	done	meet
tap	tar	pet
tip	door	fit
dump	town	rat
dark	deep	fat
talk	toad	cat
does	duty	bad
darn	told	mad
daughter	doll	mold

Lesson 22

1. Our basketball team won every game this winter.
2. I owe you a debt of gratitude for your help.
3. The hot water tap is dripping; it needs a new washer.
4. He gave the boy a generous tip.
5. Don't dump the hot ashes into a paper bag.
6. An owl sees well in the dark, not in the daylight.
7. I will talk to her and see if I can make her change her mind.
8. Does the smoke from my cigarette bother you?
9. I will darn the socks for you if you give them to me.
10. My sister has three sons and a daughter.
11. I don't think we have time to stop at the Post Office.
12. What have you done with my book? I left it on the table.
13. Fresh tar has been spread on this road. We'll have to take another way.
14. I heard the door bang. I think Harry is home.
15. We like living in a small town.
16. The stream is too deep at this point to wade across.
17. The children love to catch a toad to play with.
18. The new nurse will be on duty for the three-to-eleven shift.
19. He told me he couldn't hold the reservation for more than twenty-four hours.
20. My little girl was given a walking doll for Christmas.
21. Can you lend me a dime for the parking meter?
22. Our debating club meets twice a month.
23. You are very foolish to pet a strange dog.
24. He must have given me the wrong key; it doesn't fit the lock.
25. I think a rat has got in the cellar. I must buy a trap.
26. It is difficult to buy clothes when you are fat.
27. Please don't give me a cat. I don't like them.
28. It's too bad you can't go with us next week.
29. I'm so mad at myself for forgetting to mail this letter while I was out.
30. What flavor Jell-o mold would you like me to make?
31. It is rare to see a team of horses these days.
32. I'm not fit to go on duty with this cold.

33. It is high time this debt was paid off.
34. Please take this trash out and dump it.
35. I haven't done a darn thing all day.
36. What time will you meet me for lunch?
37. Did you think you heard a tap on the door?
38. Her daughter is too fat. She is trying to make her diet.
39. Does the team look to be in tip-top shape?
40. I'll dump my bags in the hall and take them up later.
41. He is deeply in debt and doesn't know what can be done.
42. I hope my cat will scare the rats away.
43. I went to town to talk to my lawyer.
44. Some women like to dress dolls for fairs.
45. Can you change a quarter for two dimes and a nickel? I want to phone.
46. The weather is so bad, I think I will ask you to meet me tomorrow.
47. It grows dark so early in winter and the evenings are very long.
48. I have a door stop that is a ceramic toad.

LESSON 23

The Shape of the Sound of j and Soft g

j—as in jump
soft g—as in gem

The movement is the same for the soft g, j, sh and ch. The lips are thrust forward and the opening appears rather square.

j and soft g

Syllables:
jā—jōō—joi—ger—jō—jah—gĕ—gĭ—jŭ

Syllable Drill:

sē joi	whī chā
mī joi	hōō chā
mī gĕ	hōō jah
her gĕ	mī jah
gĕ sō	Who changed my jars?
sō jŭ	
It is so just.	

Word Drill:

jolly	jest	German
jam	Jamaica	gentleman
jump	jar	germ
joke	join	ginger
jewel	January	gelatine
juice	Japanese	orange
June	just	change
July	judge	page
jury	Jerusalem	Egypt
junior	enjoy	edge
jet	genius	college
jade	gem	passage

1. We had such a jolly time when the family was here.
2. Will you make jam with your strawberries?
3. If anyone asked me to go to Japan, I would jump at the chance.
4. Did you get the point of the joke he just told?
5. An emerald is a very precious jewel.
6. I must squeeze the orange juice for breakfast.
7. Many people choose the month of June for their wedding.
8. It was a difficult case and the jury was out out for six hours.
9. One of our hottest months is July.
10. My brother is the junior partner of the firm.
11. Have you ever flown in a jet plane to Europe?
12. Some green jade is very valuable.
13. Perhaps you can go to Jamaica on a cruise this winter.
14. You will find the jar of cold cream on my dressing table.
15. Now that you live here, will you join the beach club?
16. I must not miss the January white sales.
17. The Japanese are a very artistic people.
18. I just finished reading the book you lent me.
19. Don't judge me too harshly if I make a mistake.
20. Do you enjoy going to concerts?
21. Diamonds are the gem most often used for an engagement ring.
22. I was given a German shepherd puppy for my birthday.
23. He is a gentleman in every respect.
24. A virus is a very nasty and persistent germ.
25. My grandmother used to make good gingerbread.
26. At lunch they served a lime gelatine mold with cottage cheese.
27. How much are oranges selling for in the market?
28. My friends have just returned from Jerusalem.
29. You must change trains at the next station.
30. I have marked the page where I want you to start reading.
31. Egypt is the home of the sphinx.
32. Both my children are in college this year.

Lesson 23

33. Keep back from the edge of the station platform; the train is coming.
34. Don't block the passage with boxes and crates.
35. Yes, he is a painter and really a genius.
36. Give Junior some orange gelatine.
37. Will you have tomato juice or ginger ale?
38. I don't know enough to be able to judge the merits of the plan.
39. Just don't jump to conclusions.
40. Everyone at the party was jolly and many good jokes were told.
41. Our rose garden was beautiful in June.
42. Let's join the rest of the class for the picnic.
43. I am going to see my invalid aunt and will take her two jars of jam.
44. Do you know what gem is the January birthstone?
45. Is the gentleman speaking Japanese or German?
46. I must change the date of my appointment from June to July.
47. She gave me a little carved jade elephant.
48. We went to Jamaica this year and I enjoyed the change so much.

LESSON 24

The Shape of the Sound of r After f, b, p and th

fr—as in frost
   The lower lip touches the upper teeth as for f followed quickly by the turning upward and backward movement of the tongue for r; the lips show a forward thrust.

br and pr—as in press and broad
   The lips opening from closed position as for p and b quickly followed by the r movement; the lips show a forward thrust.

thr—as in thread
   The tip of the tongue visible between the front teeth as for th quickly followed by the r movement and a forward thrust of the lip. The r movement is more clearly seen with thr than with fr, pr or br.

r after f, b, p, and th

Syllables:
        frā—froō—frī—frow—frē—froi—frah—frō—fraw
        brā—broō—brī—brow—brē—broi—brah—brō—braw
        prā—proō—prī—prow—prē—prō—prĭ—pră
        thrā—throō—thrī—thrō—thrē—thrĕ—thrŭ

Syllable Drill:

hoō fā	thrē foō
hoō bā	thē froō
thā bā	thē fō
thā brā	thā frō
thā brō	thā brō
They broke the record.	thā braw
	They brought the fruit.

Lesson 24

Word Drill:

bride	prefer	freeze	thread
breath	press	fresh	through
break	print	frame	thrive
branch	private	frost	thrift
brim	promise	free	throw
bright	prepare	front	three
broad	present	frown	throat
broom	praise	fright	thrill

Compare:

pick—prick   pay—pray
though—throw   bow—brow
bake—brake   fame—frame
bide—bride   board—broad

1. The bride wore a white veil.
2. Take a deep breath and hold it.
3. I will try not to break my promise.
4. A large branch of the tree broke off in the storm.
5. I prefer my coffee black with sugar.
6. She is going to press my dress for the party.
7. The book goes to print next month.
8. It is a private beach, so it is not crowded.
9. We must freeze the raspberries as soon as we pick them.
10. Will you get me a dozen fresh eggs at the farm?
11. The gilt frame is just right for the picture.
12. I think we will have an early frost this year.
13. The light is too poor; I can't see to thread my needle.
14. We will go through New York on our way south.
15. The boys thrive on sun and fresh air.
16. Thrift will be necessary if we are to make both ends meet.
17. The pail was full to the brim with bubbling fresh milk.
18. The sun is so bright it makes me squint.
19. The city's broad avenues are beautiful.
20. A new broom sweeps clean.
21. I promise not to disturb the papers on your desk.
22. We will prepare plenty of sandwiches for the picnic.

23. There were three hundred people present at the rally.
24. His new book received a great deal of praise from the press.
25. Now that vacation is here, I am free to come and go as I please.
26. Will you please bring the car around to the front of the house?
27. Don't frown when I ask you to practice.
28. Seeing the snake in the garden gave me a terrible fright.
29. Will you throw all these old magazines away?
30. The police station is just three miles away.
31. If you continue to speak so loudly, it will give you a sore throat.
32. It was a real thrill to watch the air show.
33. The bride was given in marriage by her father.
34. The room was so hot I had to go out for a breath of air.
35. I have lost my key and will have to break a window to get in.
36. This town is only on a branch line of the railroad.
37. Do you prefer poetry or prose?
38. The President will meet the press this afternoon.
39. The print is so small I need a magnifying glass to read it.
40. He hired a private detective to get the information.
41. The lake will soon freeze over and we can skate.
42. The boy is too fresh and should be spoken to sternly.
43. Put the picture in the frame and hang it on the wall.
44. Shall I frost the cake with chocolate or orange icing?
45. This thread is too coarse for the material.
46. He is a bright lad and I think he will go far.
47. I bought a wedding present for Nancy and Ralph.
48. You should put on an apron to protect the front of your dress.

LESSON 25

The Shape of the Sound of r After Hard c and Hard g

cr—as in crab
gr—as in grow

Hard c and g have little visible movement rapidly followed by the turning backward and upward of the tip of the tongue as for r. There is here also a forward movement of the lips. This is a bit more pronounced in the cr and gr blends than the previous group due to a time lag for the tongue to get from the c and g position to the r position.

r after hard c and hard g

Syllables:

crē—croō—crī—crou—crō—crā—crĭ—crŭ—cră
grē—groō—grī—grou—grō—grā—grĭ—grŭ—gră

Syllable Drill:

hoō că crō	thā doō
hoō că gĭ	thā mā
că thā gĭ	mā fī
wĭ thā gĭ	mā wī
wĭ gĭ crĕ	wī frŏ
Will they give you credit?	frŏ grā
	Wine is made from grapes.

Word Drill:

cream	crush	grain
crease	crew	grave
credit	cry	grown
craft	cruel	grape
cramp	crate	greet
crisp	green	grudge
crank	grate	great

crane	grind	grow
crab	ground	grist
crowd	group	greater

Compare:

cane—crane	go—grow
cowd—crowd	gate—grate
camp—cramp	gape—grape

1. Do you take cream in your coffee?
2. Don't frown. You will crease your forehead.
3. I know the shoe shop will give me credit.
4. A boat is often called a craft.
5. I have a cramp in my leg from sitting so long.
6. These cookies are nice and crisp.
7. In the old days, you had to crank a car to start it.
8. Yesterday I saw a beautiful white crane on the marsh.
9. Does a crab always walk sideways?
10. A crowd gathered when the accident happened.
11. There is a dreadful crush in the subway every night.
12. The crew of the racing sloop was carefully chosen.
13. I never heard a child cry as much as Chris does.
14. He was known to be a cruel man.
15. I received a crate of grapefruit from Florida.
16. The grass is very green for the end of summer.
17. I cleaned out the grate this morning.
18. The work is such a grind and it bores me.
19. Don't sit on the ground; the grass is wet.
20. We have a nice group of friends who dine together every Saturday.
21. I must get a bag of grain so I can feed the birds.
22. He had a very grave illness last year.
23. The grass has grown so high it must be cut soon.
24. Will you make us some grape jelly?
25. The president will greet the members of the press.
26. You must try not to bear a grudge.
27. It's a great day for the horse races.
28. Do you grow cucumbers in your garden?

Lesson 25

29. Have you ever visited a grist mill?
30. There is greater danger of accidents in bad weather.
31. These melons are the cream of the crop.
32. I have made a bad crease in my new coat.
33. Give credit where credit is due.
34. It is nice to learn a craft as a hobby.
35. Cramp the front wheels of the car if you park on a hill.
36. The air feels crisp and cool this morning.
37. I think we will have to get a crane to lift the beams.
38. This year's game drew a better crowd.
39. Some people crab all the time.
40. They crush the grapes to make wine.
41. Do you like seedless green grapes?
42. We will greet the group together.
43. Everyone says she is a crank.
44. Children love to play with an old crate.
45. My son has outgrown all his clothes this summer.
46. There isn't a grain of truth in the story.
47. It seems cruel to refuse the child a pony ride.
48. I usually grind my own coffee.

LESSON 26

The Shape of the Sound of l After f, s, b and p

fl—as in flag
    The movement of f, lower lip touching upper teeth quickly followed by the movement of l, the tip of the tongue touching the palate back of the teeth.

sl—as in slow
    The movement of s, the teeth brought close together and the lips slightly parted flowing into the movement of l.

bl—as in blame
pl—as in play
    The movement of b and p, the lips opening from a closed position flowing into the movement of l.

    These movements tend to prolong the shape of the vowel which follows them.

l after f, s, b, p

Syllables:
    flō—flī—flou—flā—floō—flē—flah—flŭ—flaw—flă—flĕ—flĭ
    slō—slī—slou—slā—sloō—slē—slah—slaw—slă—slĭ—slŭ—slĕ

Syllable Drill:

hoō floō	hē mā fī
thā floō	hoō mā fī
floō plā	thā doō fī
flī plā	thā doō slĭ
mā flĭ	hoō mā slĭ
ī mā	shē mā fī
flī plā	fī mī slĭ
I may fly the plane.	She may find my slipper.

Word Drill:

bleak	please	fleet	sleep
black	pledge	flag	slam

Lesson 26

blind	plant	float	slide
block	play	fly	slip
blow	plot	flower	slight
blue	place	floor	slow
blame	plan	flake	slant
bloom	plum	flood	slum

Compare:

back—black	bind—blind
peas—please	pan—plan
feet—fleet	four—floor
sight—slight	sow—slow

1. The old house looked bleak and deserted.
2. It is not becoming to some people to wear black.
3. You are just headed up a blind alley.
4. My sister lives only a block away.
5. Please hand me the telephone book.
6. I signed a pledge to give to the hospital.
7. I have a geranium plant on my window sill.
8. Did you enjoy the play you went to see on Saturday?
9. The yacht club has a large fleet of racing boats.
10. You should always show respect to our flag.
11. Do you like to float on your back when in swimming?
12. I hope someday to fly to Japan.
13. I couldn't sleep last night, the wind made so much noise.
14. Don't slam the door; shut it quietly.
15. Slide the bureau drawer into place.
16. Be careful not to slip on the icy steps.
17. The bad news was a blow to us all.
18. I think my favorite color is blue.
19. My roses should bloom in another week.
20. Don't try to shift the blame. The error was yours.
21. I think the bank robbers had made a careful plot.
22. What is the name of the place where your friends live?
23. I plan to take a vacation in the winter this year.
24. Will you have a plum or a pear for dessert?

25. Do you have a flower garden where you live?
26. The floor should be sanded and stained.
27. Each flake of snow is different.
28. The poor girl was in a flood of tears over her mistake.
29. The weather bureau says there is a slight chance of rain.
30. The local train is terribly slow.
31. The slant of the ramp was very steep.
32. The boy lived in a slum during his childhood.
33. What a bleak place the moor is!
34. Anemones are also called windflowers.
35. Some blind people play the piano.
36. I would rather fly, I think; the train is slow.
37. Please don't block the driveway.
38. The black paint is beginning to flake off.
39. I blame the city for the existence of slums.
40. Will you give me a slip from your ivy plant?
41. I feel very slowed up today; I had so little sleep.
42. I always like to have some blue flowers in my garden.
43. In the early spring, you may see blocks of ice floating in the river.
44. He received a slight blow on the head from the falling branch.
45. The children were looking for a place to go sliding.
46. I thought I saw a few flakes of snow.
47. Please write the sentence on the blackboard.
48. I will take the blame if the plums aren't ripe.

LESSON 27

The Shape of the Sound of l After Hard c and g

cl—as in claim
gl—as in glue

Hard c and g have no visible shape. Sometimes a slight movement of the neck muscles may be seen, but usually only the movement of the l can be seen in the combination of these consonants.

l after hard c and g

Syllables:

clā—cloō—clī—claw—clē—clō—clĭ—clŭ—clă
glā—gloō—glī—glaw—glē—glō—glĭ—glŭ—glă

Syllable drill:

I doō clă   hoō mā hă
Ī mā clă   mā thā hă
Ī mā cā   wē mā hă
hē mā cā   wē mā clē
hē mā clā   mā wē clē
hē mā clī   mā Ī clē
thā mā clī   May I have a clean glass?
They may climb the mountain.

Word Drill:

clean	clothes	club	glass
clap	claim	glance	globe
clear	clutter	glare	glue
climb	cling	glad	glasses
clip	clerk	glide	glove
clock	clover	glimpse	glaze
close	clue	glow	glitter
class	clash	gloomy	glory

Compare:

came—claim	go—glow
gaze—glaze	guide—glide
cash—clash	gad—glad
cock—clock	cap—clap

1. Will you bring me a clean towel, please?
2. Did you hear that clap of thunder?
3. The air is very clear and sparkling today.
4. I climb the mountain with my brother.
5. I must clip the hedge tomorrow.
6. This clock loses time. Will you have it regulated?
7. If you close the door, we can have more privacy to talk.
8. Many people enjoy going to a class reunion.
9. I have put my winter clothes away in moth balls.
10. He sent in a claim to his insurance company.
11. We have so much business we had to hire another clerk.
12. Clover smells sweet in the hot sun.
13. The police haven't a clue as to who committed the crime.
14. There is often a clash of wills between the father and son.
15. We have had to raise our club dues.
16. I had only time to give a glance at the paper.
17. The glare of the sun hurt my eyes.
18. We are so glad you brought your friend with you.
19. It is a pleasure to watch the skaters glide over the ice.
20. It was wonderful to at least have a glimpse of you.
21. The praise made her glow with pleasure.
22. Did you ever see such a gloomy, dark house?
23. The hostess' dinner table was set with beautiful glass.
24. He has travelled all over the globe.
25. I shall need to buy some glue to make my model plane.
26. When did you start to wear glasses?
27. I am afraid I dropped my glove in one of the shops.
28. These tiles have a beautiful glaze.
29. The glitter of the sun on the water is blinding.
30. A morning glory is a climbing vine.
31. I must clean my glasses. I can't see a thing.

Lesson 27

32. The club members clapped with enthusiasm when the speaker finished.
33. I saw him glance at me from clear across the room.
34. We climbed the stairs to bed as the clock struck twelve.
35. The glitter of a diamond clip sparkled on her shoulder.
36. We were close to despair when the news finally came.
37. I got caught in a storm on the way home, so I must change my wet clothes.
38. We hadn't a clue as to what the clash was about.
39. Do you belong to the Globe Trotters Club?
40. The glass of the mirror is badly cracked.
41. The clerk glared at me when I said I wanted to return the hat.
42. Sunday can be a very gloomy day if you are alone in a big city.
43. Be careful when you go down the steps; there is a glaze of ice.
44. Yesterday I found a five leaf clover.
45. We travelled tourist class on the ship.
46. He will justly claim the reward.
47. The children always leave a clutter of toys on the floor.
48. This vine will cling to the wall and make it look less bare.

LESSON 28

The Shape of the Sound of dr and tr

dr—as in drive
tr—as in troop.

The movement of dr and tr is the same. Unlike cr and gr, both consonants may sometimes be seen in dr and tr. The movement of d and t, the flat edge of the tongue touches the palate, lips parted and the teeth quite close together followed by the movement of r.

Syllables:

drā—drō—drī—draw—drah—drē—drōō—dră
drĭ—drŭ—drĕ—drou
trā—trō—trī—trou—trē—trōō—trĭ—trŭ
tră—trĕ—trah

Syllable Drill:

hōō dah	hē mā tĭ
wē dah	hē mā trĭ
wē drah	hē mā trŭ
hē drah	thā mā trŭ
hē drī	thā mā tră
thā drī	wē mā tră
They drive to work.	We may travel together.

Word Drill:

dream	drew	treat	troop
draft	drip	train	trade
draw	drawer	trim	tree
dress	dried	true	trail
drive	drama	trick	tried
drop	drape	trust	travel
dry	drink	trouble	trend
drain	droop	truth	trip

Lessson 28

Compare:

      dive—drive   dye—dry
      tick—trick   tea—tree
      dew—drew   deign—drain
      tail—trail   two—true

1. I couldn't remember my dream when I woke up.
2. Do you feel a draft from the window?
3. You may draw your own conclusions.
4. I have been looking for a wool dress.
5. I think I will drive to New York on Monday.
6. I am always losing things because I drop them and don't hear when they fall.
7. We have had a very hot dry, summer.
8. The kitchen drain is stopped up. I will call the plumber.
9. We drew lots to see who would have the car for the day.
10. I left the keys in my desk drawer.
11. Raisins are dried grapes.
12. My sister is studying at the drama school.
13. This material is very easy to drape.
14. What kind of drink will you have, gin or whiskey?
15. The shrubs are beginning to droop, it has been dry for so long.
16. I will treat you to lunch today.
17. My train was an hour and forty minutes late.
18. The dress is trimmed with silk braid.
19. Is the following statement true or false?
20. It was a mean trick she played on me.
21. I trust the children will not make a nuisance of themselves.
22. She seems to be always looking for trouble.
23. The truth of the matter is that I don't care for modern art.
24. We met a troop of gypsies on the road.
25. What will you trade me for this knife?
26. Have you ever followed the Appalachian trail?
27. I don't know what kind of tree it is.
28. I tried to reach you on the phone three times yesterday.

29. I hate to travel with a lot of luggage.
30. Do you follow my trend of thought?
31. We always had trouble with the drains in the old house.
32. Here is the first draft of my speech.
33. The children are driving me crazy. They have been getting into fights all day.
34. The trail is lined with dogwood trees.
35. It is a dream of mine to visit Japan.
36. I put the baby's dress in the second drawer of the dresser.
37. We dropped in on John and Mary the other evening.
38. We tried to catch the nine o'clock train but missed it.
39. I got a good trade-in on my old car.
40. Will you trust me to drive your car to Boston?
41. The trouble is I am drooping with fatigue.
42. The circus parade always has a large troop of elephants.
43. He drew a pencil portrait of my aunt.
44. Is the dinner a dress affair?
45. Will you help me to hang these drapes?
46. Is that a drip dry shirt you are wearing?
47. I wish you would go on the trip with me.
48. Don't try to trick me; I know you haven't practiced.

LESSON 29

The Shape of the Sound of sm, sp and sw Before a Vowel

sm—as in smoke
sp—as in spoil

The movement of s, teeth brought close together, lips slightly parted followed by the movement of m and p, the lips opening from a closed position.

sw—as in swim

The movement of s followed by the movement of w, lips forward or puckered.

*sm, sp and sw
before a vowel*

Syllables:

spō—spōō—spī—spou—spā—spoi—spē—spah
spaw—spĭ—spĕ
smō—smōō—smī—smaw—smah—smŭ—smĕ
swō—swōō—swī—swē—swah—swā—swĭ—swĕ

Syllable Drill:

thā smah	hōō spē	hē swah
wē smah	hōō spā	wē swah
wē smō	shă spā	wē saw
hē smō	shă spoi	thā saw
hē smī	thā spoi	thā saw swah
hē smah	spoi fŭ	wē saw swah
He is very smart.	They will spoil the fun.	We saw the swan.

Word Drill:

smart	spell	spoke	sworn
smoke	spirit	space	sweep
small	sport	spade	swipe

87

smile	span	spoil	sweet
smooth	spare	spend	swan
smell	speak	spill	swamp
spine	spark	swollen	swell
spatter	spool	swore	swim

Compare:

soak—smoke soothe—smooth
soil—spoil seat—sweet
sore—swore search—smirch
sell—spell send—spend

1. The boy is smart. He will go far.
2. Smoke and fog are called smog.
3. Their house is small and very cozy.
4. Her smile is so warm and friendly.
5. The sea is very smooth today and there is no wind.
6. Try not to spatter the pedestrians when you drive on a wet day.
7. The boy's spine was injured in an automobile accident.
8. The smell of stew cooking is delicious.
9. I am afraid this spell of good weather won't last much longer.
10. In spite of his handicap, he has a great deal of spirit.
11. He has had so much trouble in a short span of time.
12. Did you look to see if the spare tire needs air?
13. The president will speak tonight on domestic affairs.
14. I think I will need new spark plugs.
15. My spool rolled under the sofa and I can't reach it.
16. I spoke to him about taking the position.
17. It would terrify me to fly into outer space.
18. We hired a man to spade the vegetable garden for us.
19. It's dreadful the way they spoil the child.
20. I don't want to spend too much for a coat.
21. My ankles are swollen from standing so long.
22. I swore I would never go near that shop again.
23. Our new town clerk was sworn in this morning.
24. He won the election in a clean sweep.

25. These Concord grapes we bought yesterday are very sweet.
26. I will try to swipe a pencil from somebody.
27. A swan at close quarters can be a very dangerous bird.
28. This morning I saw a hunter with his gun walking in the marsh.
29. The small boat bobbed in the swell of the ocean.
30. Do you think you could swim a hundred yards?
31. My hand is swollen and smarts from the wasp sting.
32. I like the smell of the burning leaves, but the smoke gets in my eyes.
33. I am sworn to secrecy about their honeymoon plans.
34. There is space for thirty spools in my sewing box.
35. Lower the heat under the pan so the grease won't spatter.
36. This mystery story is really spine chilling.
37. He doesn't give me his attention when I speak to him.
38. A car nearly sideswiped me on the road and I swore at the man.
39. A swan has made her nest in the swamp.
40. The girl has a very sweet spirit and she is completely unspoiled.
41. Smile and the world smiles with you.
42. Be smart and don't speak too soon.
43. I spend my spare time writing.
44. He spoke to me about the smoke pollution.
45. Don't use your hand so much. Give the swelling a chance to go down.
46. You should be a good sport even when you lose.
47. Take care. Don't spill the coffee on the papers.
48. The fruit will spoil if you don't pick it soon.

LESSON 30

The Shape of the Sound of st, sk and sc (hard c) Before a Vowel

st—as in steep
 The movement of s, teeth brought close together, lips slightly parted followed rapidly by the movement of t, flat edge of tongue touching the palate, lips parted.

sk—as in skip
s (hard)c—as in scold
 The movement of s followed by the invisible movement of k and hard c.

st, sk and sc (hard c) before a vowel

Syllables:
 stā—stōō—stī—stou—stē—stah—stō—staw—stĕ—stĭ—stŭ—stă
 skā—skōō—skī—scou—skē—scah—scō—scaw—skĭ—skŭ—scă

Syllable Drill:

wē dōō stō	hou scă
wē dōō stā	hou scō
thā dōō stā	hou skā
hōō dŭz stā	hou thā
hōō dŭz stŭ	hou thŭ
dōō yōō stŭ	hou thŭ lē
Do you study hard?	How the leaves scatter.

Word Drill:

steep	stern	stale	scatter
stack	stove	scold	skirt
stage	star	skate	scope
stand	stamp	sky	scald
store	still	skill	scare

90

Lesson 30

stall	style	scant	score
steam	stew	skip	ski
study	stuck	skunk	scale

Compare:

    sack—stack   sore—store
    seam—steam   sand—stand
    sigh—sky   seep—steep
    sold—scold   sip—skip

1. The road was so steep, I was out of breath from the climb.
2. I have a stack of unpaid bills on my desk.
3. Did you ever think of going on the stage?
4. Don't stand there doing nothing.
5. Will you go to the store for me? I need some flour.
6. Isn't it maddening when you stall the car in traffic?
7. The children have to run and yell to let off steam.
8. I must go home and study for my exam.
9. The teacher was very stern with the children.
10. Oil stoves are very dangerous. They cause many fires.
11. It's still raining hard. We better wait a little longer before leaving.
12. I don't think the dress is quite my style.
13. A good hot stew is just the thing for a cold day.
14. My car was stuck in the snow and had to be pulled out.
15. You should give the stale bread to the birds.
16. She will scold me if I break another plate.
17. I learned to skate when I was about seven years old.
18. There is not a cloud in the sky today.
19. He looked at my attempt to paint with scorn.
20. They say there is scant hope of finding the men alive.
21. Please don't skip your practicing.
22. Some people say that a skunk makes a nice pet.
23. Don't scatter the leaves that I have just raked up.
24. I am afraid that my skirt is too long for the fashion.
25. We didn't realize the scope of the problem.
26. Be careful not to knock over the pot or you will scald yourself.

27. She tried to scare me with her predictions.
28. What is the score in the tournament match?
29. There are many popular ski runs in New England.
30. If you want to help me, you could scale the fish.
31. There is scant chance of my being able to go with you.
32. Will you stack the plates for me in the cupboard?
33. He is always so stern, he scares me.
34. Be careful. The steam from the car radiator might scald you.
35. Put the fish on the scales; let's see how much it weighs.
36. This is a fine day to skate; let's skip class.
37. My new skirt is the latest style.
38. Light the stove for me while I scatter this bread for the birds.
39. When I go to the store, I will scold the clerk for cheating me.
40. I left the toothpaste on the washstand.
41. I think we will have stewed fruit for dessert.
42. What new subject will you study this year?
43. Her paintings show a great deal of skill and promise.
44. I prefer a stage play to the movies.
45. He couldn't help the mistake. Don't scold him.
46. What is your usual score for nine holes of golf?
47. I don't see a single star tonight.
48. Could you lend me an airmail stamp?

LESSON 31

The Shape of the Sound of str, scr and spr Before a Vowel

str—as in street

The movement of s, teeth close together, lips slightly parted followed rapidly by the movement of t, flat edge of tongue touching palate, flowing into the movement of r; here the tip of the tongue descends slightly from the palate, where it was for t, and returns toward the palate. The lips remain slightly open throughout the movements of the three consonants.

scr—as in scrape

The movement of s, followed by the invisible movement of hard c, followed by the movement of r, tip of tongue turned upward and backward toward the palate. Lips remaining open throughout.

spr—as in spring

The movement of s followed rapidly by the movement of p, lips opening from a closed position followed by the movement of r, tip of tongue turned upward and backward toward the palate.

*str, scr and spr
before a vowel*

Syllables:

Strō—strā—strōō—strē—strī—straw—strĕ—stră
scrōō—scrā—scrē—scraw—scră—scrŭ
sprōō—sprā—sprē—sprou—sprī—spraw—sprĕ—sprĭ

Syllable Drill:

mā strā	how scō	thā mā spō
thā strā	wē scrō	hē dĭ spō
thā strī	wē her	hē dĭ sprē

Lipreading

 how strī hōō her shē mā sprē
 how strē hōō scrē shē saw sprē
 thē strē ā scrē shē saw sprōō
 The street was Who heard a wē saw sprōō
  deserted. scream? We saw a blue spruce.

Word Drill:

string	strong	screen	sprout
strain	strip	scrap	spring
stroll	stretch	scream	spruce
straight	strength	scramble	sprawl
strike	scrape	scruples	spritely
street	scratch	screech	sprain
strive	scrub	scrim	sprat
strap	screw	spread	spray

1. I will tie a string around my finger so as to not to forget.
2. Trying to listen when you can't hear is a great strain.
3. Sunday was a beautiful day and the whole family went for a stroll.
4. A straight line is the shortest distance between two points.
5. They say there is going to be a railroad strike.
6. Our street is very dark and should have more street lights.
7. Strive as I may, it is difficult to make both ends meet.
8. I broke the strap of my wrist watch and must get another.
9. My niece isn't at all strong. She has to be very careful.
10. The children always beg for the comic strip of the Sunday paper.
11. We must have the strength to face disaster if it comes.
12. The boys are always getting into a scrape of some sort.
13. I am afraid I have made a scratch on your new table.
14. I never have liked brussel sprouts.
15. I had to scrub the kitchen floor. It was covered with muddy prints.
16. Will you screw the cap on the jar, please?
17. The window screen fell out and nearly struck a woman passing below.
18. There is not a scrap of truth in the story she told.

Lesson 31

19. Sometimes I could scream when the children have been quarreling all day.
20. It is such a scramble to get things ready for the fair.
21. I think he has few scruples and would do anything for money.
22. I heard a screech owl last night and the sound was eery.
23. She bought new scrim curtains for her bedroom.
24. Will you spread the butter on the bread for me?
25. My crocuses are beginning to sprout and they are spreading everywhere.
26. I wish spring would come. I am so tired of snow and ice.
27. We just planted a blue spruce in front of the house.
28. Teenagers never sit; they sprawl.
29. Don't you think she is very spritely for her age?
30. I received a very nasty sprain when I twisted my ankle.
31. A sprat is a very small fish.
32. Naturally, you will scream if I strike you.
33. Unfortunately he broke the strap of my valise.
34. A strong wind blew the rain along the city streets.
35. We must scrape off the old paint before we can start to do the chair.
36. A string of Japanese lanterns lit the patio.
37. You must strive to do better or you won't pass your exam.
38. Did you sprain your ankle or just strain it?
39. We went straight to the police station to report the accident.
40. Would you like scrambled eggs for breakfast?
41. My new bedspread is made of green silk.
42. I think the spring of the lock is broken.
43. Her hair is straight and she wears it short.
44. It will take the strength of two men to lift the dresser.
45. They have a color TV with a wide screen.
46. She screeched when the mouse ran across the room.
47. This is a very lonely stretch of road.
48. Don't you think we had better spray the roses again?

LESSON 32

The Shape of the Sound of sl and sn Before a Vowel

sl—as in slate.

The movement of s, followed rapidly by the movement of l, tip of the tongue touching the palate just back of the upper teeth; the movement is seen as the tongue descends.

sn—as in snow

The movement of s followed by the almost unseen movement of n.

*sl and sn
before a vowel*

Syllables:

slā—slō—slī—slōō—slaw—slă—slĭ—slŭ—slĕ
snā—snō—snē—snāh—snī—snōō—snă—snĭ—snŭ

Syllable Drill:

hōō ĭs slō	thā saw snah
he ĭs slō	hōō saw snah
ĭs hē slō	hōō saw snē
ĭs hē slĕ	hē saw snē
hē ĭs slĕ	hē saw snā
shē ĭs slĕ	thā saw snā
She is a slender girl.	wē saw snā
	We saw the snake coil.

Word Drill:

slate	sliver	snarl	sneeze
slow	slacken	snow	snake
slide	slap	snare	sniper
sloop	slight	snooze	snub
slam	slaw	snort	snuggle

Lesson 32

slip	slicker	snack	sneer
slump	sleep	snip	snap
sled	slender	sneak	snatch

Compare:

sew—slow   sort—snort
soup—sloop   seek—sneak
sip—slip   sake—snake
said—sled   sap—snap

1. A slate roof is a good precaution against fire.
2. Business is slow now that the holidays are over.
3. This bureau drawer won't slide. I must rub soap on it.
4. Do you know how many masts a sloop has?
5. Please don't slam the screen door when you go out.
6. Be careful not to slip. The sidewalk is very icy.
7. There has been a serious slump in the stock market.
8. When I was a child, I used a sled that had belonged to my uncle.
9. Please cut me a sliver of this cheese so that I may sample it.
10. We will have to slacken our speed as we near town.
11. I have a slight headache. I think my glasses should be changed.
12. Will you have some cole slaw with your hamburger?
13. A fisherman's raincoat is called a slicker.
14. When I go to bed, I have to read before I can get to sleep.
15. I wish I was as slender as I used to be.
16. My shoe lace is in such a snarl, I will have to cut it.
17. Are they predicting another snowstorm or just rain?
18. I set a trap to try to snare a woodchuck that is eating my garden.
19. Many people like to take a snooze after Sunday dinner.
20. Don't snort when I make a statement. I know what I am talking about.
21. We stopped for a snack on our way home from the movies.
22. Will you snip this thread for me with your scissors?
23. I will sneak in and see if the baby is asleep.
24. My hayfever makes me sneeze continually.

25. Some people like a snake for a pet. The idea makes me shiver.
26. The man was killed by a sniper on the roof of a building.
27. She tried to snub my friend and I told her what I thought of her.
28. Every morning the puppy wakes me trying to snuggle up in my bed.
29. I am afraid he will sneer at my offer of help.
30. Will you have a ginger snap with your tea?
31. He slammed the book on the table and walked out.
32. A state tax will soon be on the political slate.
33. Don't slump in your chair. Didn't you get enough sleep?
34. I think the rain has slackened; we could go now.
35. He is a vicious dog and will snarl and snap if you approach him.
36. Did he try to snare you with his free offer?
37. There is a new snack bar across from the theater.
38. You must always cover your face when you are going to sneeze.
39. There is a slight difference in the size of the two volumes.
40. A slicker is usually made of yellow oilskin.
41. The meat is sliced so thin, it is in slivers.
42. I bought three slips when they had their sale.
43. There is a bad bend in the road ahead. Go slow and blow the horn.
44. He wants to go out and slide in the snow.
45. We are going to cruise to Bermuda on my brother's sloop.
46. I wanted to slap the boy, he was so fresh.
47. I have just time to snatch a sandwich before the train arrives.
48. The old dog lay snoozing in the sun.

LESSON 33

The Shape of the Sound of q and sq Before a Vowel

q—as in queen

q is always followed by the vowel u. The shape of the sound of qu is made up of two sounds, k and wh. The movement of k has no visible shape. The air is expelled when the sound is made in the throat. In some people a slight movement of the muscles of the neck may be visible. The sound of k is followed rapidly by the movement of wh, the lips puckered and with a forward movement.

sq—as in square

The movement of s, teeth brought close together, lips slightly parted followed by the movement of qu or k-wh, the jaw is seen to drop.

q and sq

Syllables:

quā—quī—quō—quē—quaw—quĭ—quĕ—quā
squaw—squī—squē—squā—squĭ—squĕ

Syllable Drill:

wē cō	wē saw
wē cā	thā saw
hē cā	thā sĭ
hē quā	hoō sĭ
wē quō	hoō squĭ
Ī quō	thē squĭ
I quoted the Quaker.	We saw the squirrel.

Word Drill:

quote	quart	square
quake	quota	squeak

Quebec	Quaker	squire
quiet	queer	squirrel
qualify	quartet	squad
question	quarrel	squeeze
quotation	quip	squall
quaint	quantity	squash
queen	quarter	squander
quite	quick	squelch

1. I don't want the newspaper to quote me.
2. Did you ever have the misfortune to feel an earthquake?
3. Last year we went to Quebec for winter sports.
4. Naturally a library must be a very quiet place.
5. Do you qualify for aid from the Veterans' Administration?
6. I question whether or not the plan will work.
7. Can you tell me where that quotation came from?
8. Her costume for the ball was very quaint and charming.
9. My niece was queen of the Cherry Blossom Festival this year.
10. It's not quite time for us to leave.
11. I think I am going to need another quart of milk.
12. Aliens come into this country on the quota system.
13. William Penn was a Quaker.
14. It's very queer that he hasn't called me back.
15. Next week we are going to a concert by a noted string quartet.
16. I do wish the children wouldn't quarrel so much.
17. It was an amusing quip and everybody laughed.
18. I shall need a quantity of cartons to pack for our move.
19. She paid five dollars and a quarter for the gloves.
20. If you are quick, you can catch Alice. She just went out the door.
21. A whole city square was blocked off because of the fire.
22. These new shoes of mine certainly squeak.
23. I must trap the squirrel. He is destroying my bird feeders.
24. He is quite the country squire these days.
25. A squad of police were on hand in case of trouble.
26. When washing a drip dry garment, never squeeze or twist.
27. The sailboat capsized in the squall.
28. Will you have summer squash as a vegetable?

29. He will squander every penny he gets in no time.
30. My shoes are so full of water that they squelch when I walk.
31. It was a question of who was right in the quarrel
32. She could not qualify as a beauty queen.
33. I recognized the quotation from Shakespeare at once.
34. We put up eight quarts of tomatoes.
35. She is lucky to live in such a quiet quarter.
36. In Quebec the policemen wear fur hats in winter.
37. My brother plays squash at the Athletic Club every Saturday.
38. It's a question of whether we should make the trip by plane or boat.
39. You can't fit a square peg into a round hole.
40. I had to squelch the boy because he was so fresh.
41. Everyone has their quota of troubles.
42. It was a very queer question for her to ask me.
43. I'm not quite sure if I want a square or oval frame for the picture.
44. If you remain very quiet, the squirrel will come close to you.
45. Will you squeeze a quart of orange juice for me?
46. The noise of the shooting made me quake with fright.
47. The restaurant we went to was very quaint and the food was good.
48. Now you can quit worrying. The lesson is over for today.

LESSONS 34 through 45

Words Beginning With a Vowel or Diphthong

The shape of the sounds are the same as when used in a word. However, at the beginning of a word the sound is a little more prolonged.

LESSON 34

Words Beginning With Long ā

Syllables:
        ās—ād—ām—āl—āk—āv—āp—ār—āg—ān

Syllable Drill:

Hē āl	Shē is ām
Hē wāl	Hoō is ām
Shē wāk	Hoō is tām
Ī wāk	Hoō is ān
Ī āk	Shē is ān
I have an earache.	She is an angel.

Word Drill:

ace	ale	airmail
aid	age	alien
aim	acorn	amen
ail	airplane	amiable
ache	acre	angel
aviary	aerial	April
ape	agent	Asia
ate	eight	Amos
air	aigret	Ada
apex	airless	Asa

Compare:

ace—pace	air—fair
aid—paid	ate—date
aim—lame	ail—tale
age—wage	ache—sake

1. I held an ace and three queens in my hand.
2. Are you going to buy a new hearing aid?
3. He took aim and fired.
4. She is so cranky. I don't know what ails her.

105

5. I ache all over from the unaccustomed exercise.
6. I used to have thirty birds; quite an aviary!
7. He tries to ape his father.
8. The patient ate a good meal and feels better.
9. The pollution in the air gives many people sinus trouble.
10. He is at the apex of his career and deserves credit.
11. Did you read the book, "Cakes and Ale?"
12. The boy is at a very difficult age and is hard to manage.
13. From a little acorn grows a mighty oak.
14. I have never been up in an airplane, but hope to fly someday.
15. The house has an acre of land and is well landscaped.
16. I must call the repair man. There is something wrong with my aerial.
17. He is an agent for Eastern Airlines.
18. They left a little after eight this morning.
19. Aigret feathers aren't used to trim hats anymore.
20. The room is very airless. Would you open the window, please?
21. I sent the letter airmail and hope he will get it tomorrow.
22. An alien must report his address every year.
23. The last word of a prayer is amen.
24. He is always amiable and pleasant to talk to.
25. Would you be an angel and fetch my coat for me?
26. We are going to Asia in April.
27. Did you ever listen to the Amos and Andy show?
28. I have two nieces, Ada and Alice.
29. Asa is a very old biblical name.
30. Amos was very amiable when I asked him to change the tire.
31. This seems to be the age of revolt.
32. I will get all the aid I need from my agent.
33. The squirrel sat on the aerial with an acorn in his mouth.
34. The largest continent in the world in Asia.
35. In April I traveled to Sweden by airplane.
36. You ate the angel cake. Was it good?
37. My Irish setter had eight puppies last week.
38. What ails the world? There is no peace anywhere.

39. I bought five more acres of land and will build a swimming pool.
40. Ada is an alien. She came to this country about two years ago.
41. The ape ate twenty-five bananas.
42. I don't think he will get the letter in time unless you send it airmail.
43. My brother was a flying ace in World War II.
44. In hot weather I like a tall glass of good, cold ale.
45. There's a storm in the air. I can feel it.
46. That airless room has given me a headache.
47. May I ask you to aid a good and worthy cause?
48. It's my aim to teach you to lip-read.

LESSON 35

Words Beginning With a Long ō

Syllables:

ōd—ōk—ōn—ōl—ōv—ōm—ōr—ōp—ōs—ōt—ōb—ōw

Syllable Drill:

ōr—frō	plēē—ōd—dah
ōs—frō	plēē—ōm—dah
ōs—frī	plēē—ōm—dō
ōs—frĕ	plēē—ōk—dō
ōl—frĕ	plēē—ōp—dō
Old friends are best.	Please open the door.

Word Drill:

open	oak	occasion
old	only	Oklahoma
over	oaf	obey
own	odor	oblige
omen	ore	okay
oat	oval	offense
oath	Orient	opal
ogre	Ohio	open
ode	oar	opinion
oriole	omit	oppose

Compare:

old—poled	ode—road	owe—row
own—sown	oath—both	oaf—loaf
oat—goat	ore—core	oat—moat

1. Will you open a can of soup for our lunch?
2. There is nothing so comfortable as an old jacket.
3. There has been a lot of water over the dam since we last met.
4. She is bound she will have her own way.

Lesson 35

5. Do you think Friday the thirteenth a bad omen?
6. I usually eat oatmeal for breakfast.
7. He became a citizen and took the oath of allegiance yesterday.
8. Children always like to be frightened by an ogre.

9. I have never tried to write an ode. Have you?
10. An oriole has her nest in my apple tree.
11. I saw a beautiful oak chest at my friend's house last week.
12. Friday will be the only day I can go.

13. The man was an oaf and very awkward.
14. There was a delicious odor of baking coming from the kitchen.
15. What kind of ore does the mine produce?
16. She has a beautiful oval table that belonged to her grandmother.
17. We import a great deal from the Orient.
18. Were you staying with friends while in Ohio?
19. I have dropped an oar overboard and am trying to reach it.
20. Please don't omit your practicing.

21. For what occasion are you giving your son a watch?
22. Oklahoma produces a great deal of corn and grain.
23. You must obey the traffic laws or you will be fined.
24. I shall be obliged to see my lawyer tomorrow.

25. Would it be okay with you to postpone our trip until next week?
26. I don't think your license should be suspended on a first offense.
27. The opal is a semiprecious stone.
28. I heard that you are going to open a dress shop.

29. What is your opinion of the club's new project?
30. He will oppose any plan you offer.
31. Superstitious people are always looking for an omen.
32. I'm going over to my sister's but will be back shortly.

33. An oval frame is rather old-fashioned.
34. A young fellow must sow his wild oats.
35. The oriole is a migratory bird.
36. There is a large, sturdy oak tree on my property.

37. The children must be taught to obey when spoken to.
38. In your opinion, is it wise to give teen-agers so much freedom?
39. The occasion demands a big celebration.
40. If only I could find my wallet; it contains all my papers.
41. In the old days life was much simpler.
42. Remember you are under oath to speak the truth.
43. I will be much obliged if you will post the letter for me.
44. He used an oar to push the boat out from the dock.
45. Horses like a nice bag of oats for dinner.
46. I have gone over my list and can't think of anyone I have omitted.
47. He wore an Oriental costume to the party.
48. In my own opinion, he was wrong to leave the job.

LESSON 36

Words Beginning With Long ē

Syllables:

ēb—ēd—ēk—ēl—ēv—ēn—ēz—ēt—ēr—ēb

Syllable Drill:

whī—ēb	I saw an ēb
whī—ēn	I saw an ēl
thā—ēn	I saw the ēl
thā—ēt	I saw the ēd
whī—ēt	I saw the ēk
whī—ēr	I saw the ēz
thĭ—ēr	I saw the ēg
This is a difficult era.	I saw the eagle.

Word Drill:

eat	eager	equilibrium
even	eagle	equip
eel	East	era
eke	event	eternal
enough	evenly	evangelist
ease	Easter	eve
ear	easy	easterly
elastic	eaves	egotistical
either	ego	evening
each	equator	easily

Compare:

eat—wheat	ear—tear	each—peach
either—neither	eke—beak	era—nearer
event—relent	ease—seize	eel—feel

1. May I eat lunch with you?
2. I have tried to give us all an equal share of the pie.
3. The men are fishing through holes in the ice for eel.
4. They are trying to eke out their income to cover all expenses.

5. Enough of such nonsense! You know you are not shy.
6. Take your time and be at ease. We don't have to leave for an hour.
7. Don't put your ear to the keyhole; you may hear no good of yourself.
8. Will you give me an elastic band to put around these papers?
9. At our house, it's either a feast or a famine.
10. Each and every person is entitled to their own opinion.
11. I am eager for my brother to arrive. We haven't seen each other for years.
12. The eagle is king of the birds.
13. Next month I am going East to visit my parents.
14. In the event of an air raid, do you know where to take shelter?
15. It's too bad the world's goods can't be more evenly distributed.
16. Have you bought your Easter bonnet yet?
17. It's not always easy to know what to do.
18. There are long icicles hanging from the eaves of the house.
19. She has a terrific ego and is sure she is always right.
20. Have you ever crossed the equator and been given a ducking?
21. I became dizzy and lost my equilibrium.
22. Let's raise some money to equip the team.
23. This is most certainly an era of unrest.
24. There is an eternal flame burning at the tomb of the unknown soldier.
25. Billy Graham is an evangelist.
26. It is the eve of our departure for Europe.
27. There is an easterly wind blowing. I think it will rain.
28. He is a very egotistical person. He thinks only of himself.
29. Will you go with me to the concert this evening?
30. It's easily the most important job he has ever held.
31. If you have trouble with your leg, perhaps an elastic stocking would help.
32. We must go to town tomorrow even it it snows.

33. If you each do your share of the work, we'll soon be finished.
34. Were you eavesdropping at what was being said at the next table?
35. You either like brussel sprouts or you don't.
36. We are giving a big party New Year's Eve.
37. A good golfer seems to hit the ball with such ease.
38. The man is as slippery as an eel. Beware of him!
39. I know what I said to him went in one ear and out the other.
40. My friend has a carved wooden eagle over her fireplace.
41. Have you ever eaten eel? Some people like it very much.
42. The equipment at the camp was very poor.
43. Please spread the gravel evenly in the driveway.
44. I think Ethan will be an easy winner in the tournament.
45. Each day that passes brings us closer to vacation.
46. In the event of snow tomorrow, I will meet you on Tuesday.
47. I am afraid his health isn't equal to such heavy work.
48. There are always beautiful flowers sold at Easter.

LESSON 37

Words Beginning With Long ī

Syllables:

īb—īd—īk—īl—īm—īr—īs—īt—īv

Syllable Drill:

hoō īb	hē are īr
thā—īb	wē are īr
thā—īs	thā are īv
mī—īs	thā are īk
mī—īd	thā are īd
He is my idol.	They are identical.

Word Drill:

ice	italics	Irish
I'd	I'm	identical
I've	idea	Iceland
I'll	idol	ibis
icon	item	idle
ivory	itinerary	Iowa
iron	island	identify
isolated	ideal	iris
aisle	Ireland	ivy
Idaho	icicle	itinerant

Compare:

ād—ōd—ēd—īd   āk—ōk—ēk—īk
ām—ōm—ēm—īm   ār—ōr—ēr—īr
āv—ōv—ēv—īv   ān—ōn—ēn—īn

1. Will you have some more ice in your drink?
2. I'd like to buy the picture if I could afford it.
3. I'll read your book as soon as I have finished this one.
4. Certain religious pictures are called icons.

Lesson 37

5. I am sorry. We are all out of Ivory Flakes.
6. As soon as my iron is hot, I'll get this pressing done.
7. They live in a very isolated community and see few people.
8. The bride walked up the aisle on the arm of her father.
9. Potatoes are grown in Idaho.
10. Most children love to suck an icicle.
11. His grandfather was born in Ireland.
12. The weather has been ideal all week.
13. Did you go to the island for your vacation this year?
14. I'll mail you a copy of the itinerary of the trip so you can keep in touch.
15. There was an item in the paper yesterday about the Theater for the Deaf.
16. John Barrymore was a famous screen idol.
17. Do you have any idea what I did with my gloves?
18. I don't know if I'm going to the meeting tonight.
19. The instructions are written below in italics.
20. In winter I sometimes like a nice Irish stew.
21. My cousins are identical twins.
22. They do a great business in packing fish in Iceland.
23. The ibis was considered a sacred bird in ancient Egypt.
24. I hate to sit with my hands idle. It makes me nervous.
25. Iowa is her native state. I think she was born there.
26. Were you able to identify the man in the line-up?
27. There are so many lovely shades of iris to choose from.
28. It's very easy to train ivy on a wall.
29. The Fuller brushman is an itinerant salesman.
30. The river is frozen and the ice is thick enough for skating.
31. The studio had an old-fashioned, potbellied iron stove.
32. They own the island where they have their summer home.
33. The irony of the matter is that I fell for the man's story.
34. I wish the boy would get a job; he is always idle.
35. I was asked to identify the ring that was stolen from me.
36. My iris were beautiful last spring.
37. They say the Irish love a fight.
38. Ivy will grow well even in the shade.

39. You feel so isolated when you haven't a car.
40. I've an idea Albert wants to change his job.
41. I'm sure this is the identical ring to the one I lost.
42. They are going to Iowa to visit cousins.
43. The automobile club will map the itinerary of your trip for you.
44. Italics is a sloping type of print.
45. The arrangement is ideal. I will be only a block from where I work.
46. The church had an unusually long aisle.
47. I'll give him an ivory paper cutter for Christmas.
48. Jack is his young cousin's idol.

LESSON 38

Words Beginning With Long ū—ōō—yōō—eū

Syllables:
    yōōn–yōōs–yōōt–yōōl–yōōv–yōōd–yōōr–yōōk

Syllable Drill:

Ī–pl̥oi–yōōn	thā–mō–yōōd
hē–pl̥oi–yōōl	thā–mā–yōōv
hē–plē–yōōt	wē–mā–yōōn
hē–plā–yōōk	wē–mŭ–yōōn
He plays the ukulele.	We must unite.

Word Drill:

ooze	eulogy	union
unite	usage	unique
Yule	you've	unison
use	unit	university
Europe	Ukraine	useless
utility	ukulele	universal
usual	unanimous	usurp
unity	uniform	utensil
you'd	unify	yew
useful	unilateral	youth

Compare:

ooze–choose	youth–tooth
yule–mule	useless–juiceless
yew–two	utility–futility
you've–move	use–ruse

1. Don't walk there. The mud will ooze into your shoes.
2. We must unite to make our opinion felt.
3. The Yule log burned brightly on Christmas eve.
4. Can you use a telephone satisfactorily?

5. Many Americans go to Europe in the summer.
6. Electricity is a utility; so is water.
7. It's usual for us to have a long winter.
8. There is complete unity in the party.
9. I know you'd be happy if your daughter would come for a visit.
10. A second car in a family is very useful.
11. Julian made the eulogy at his friend's funeral.
12. That word is not in current usage.
13. I'm afraid you've missed your bus.
14. A dime is a unit of our currency.
15. Have you still some family living in the Ukraine?
16. The ukelele used to be a popular instrument with teen-agers.
17. The vote was unanimous for building a skating rink.
18. A uniform is becoming to many young men.
19. They are trying to unify the country.
20. I am afraid there is only a unilateral desire for the abolishment of war.
21. The union has called a strike of oil workers.
22. The situation was unique to say the least.
23. The children sang in unison "Happy Birthday to You."
24. Which university is your son going to?
25. It's useless to try to find a taxi in this rain.
26. I believe the longing for peace is universal among all people.
27. The king's nephew is trying to usurp the throne.
28. The blender is a very useful household utensil.
29. There are usually many yew trees in a cemetery.
30. I passed a youth on the road thumbing a ride.
31. You'd find the knife more useful if you sharpened it.
32. In union there is strength.
33. The approval was unanimous.
34. He gave me the usage of his car while he is away.
35. The blood oozed from the cut on his forehead.
36. Have you visited the United Nations?
37. They usually come to see me on Sunday.
38. What a unique gift they gave you!

39. I hear your husband is teaching at the University.
40. Do you know how to use the typewriter?
41. The first unit of the new apartment complex is finished.
42. It's not usual for a youth to want to stay home every evening.
43. They will be in Europe for five months.
44. The present spirit of unrest seems to be universal.
45. Where you work do they belong to a union?
46. The yew tree is an evergreen.
47. A cat chasing a dog is an unusual sight.
48. You would find lipreading more useful if you would practice more.

LESSON 39

Words Beginning With ah

Syllables:
    ahb—ahk—ahf—ahd—ahm—aht—ahg

Syllable Drill:

thā ōb	sō ahm
thā āb	sō ahf
thā ahb	hē ahf
hoō ahb	dō ahf
hoō aht	dō ahb
hē aht	dō ahg
He is an artist.	Don't argue.

Word Drill:

art	arm	architect
ardent	afterward	arctic
Arthur	Arkansas	are
after	argeratum	Argentina
arbor	arbutous	argue
ark	artist	armaments
army	arcade	artery
arthritis	arch	armistice
arsenal	arduous	article
artistic	archaic	architecture

Compare:

ark—park	ark—lark	are—car
art—start	art—part	article—particle
arm—farm	arm—palm	are—tar
	arbor—harbor	
	arch—larch	
	artist—tartest	

Lesson 39

1. Did you study history of art in school?
2. The president made an ardent plea for unity.
3. I can't get Arthur to go to a dance.
4. After the long, dreary winter, this warm sun feels good.
5. We grow grapes over an arbor in our garden.
6. They call their boat "The Ark" because it looks so clumsy.
7. Mary's husband is an army officer, a colonel, I think.
8. I am so sorry for her; she is so crippled by arthritis.
9. There is an arsenal just outside of town.
10. Edward is very artistic; he paints beautifully.
11. I have had my arm in a cast for three weeks.
12. Let's finish the work. Afterward we will go for coffee.
13. We had two flat tires driving through Arkansas.
14. There is a small mauve flower called argeratum.
15. Arbutus grows in the woods and it is forbidden to pick it.
16. An artist is usually a temperamental person.
17. I always enjoy the shops in the arcade.
18. I have been having trouble with the arch of my left foot.
19. Making out one's income tax is an arduous job.
20. Their bookkeeping system is archaic; they should modernize it.
21. My nephew is studying to become an architect.
22. We certainly have had arctic winds blowing these past few days.
23. You are very early for your appointment.
24. We import much tinned beef from Argentina.
25. No matter what I ask him to do, he always has to argue about it.
26. I hope someday we can cease the armaments race.
27. This is the main artery for traffic through to Boston.
28. Do you have hope that an armistice will be declared soon?
29. Carl has written an article for the paper. It will be published Sunday.
30. What is the type of architecture of the new court house?
31. When the thieves were caught, they had quite an arsenal in their car.
32. When Arthur goes to Argentina on a business trip, I will go with him.

33. We planted argeratum as a border to the flower bed.
34. I will argue the point with you at another moment.
35. She was very ardent in her praise of the work accomplished.
36. Trees are usually planted on Arbor Day.
37. If you sever an artery, you may bleed to death.
38. Shall we have lunch in the arcade tea room?
39. After all the fuss she made, now she doesn't want to go on the trip.
40. The girl and boy strolled arm in arm along the beach.
41. They didn't realize the danger of the situation until afterwards.
42. Are you interested in the art of the country?
43. I don't think he has ever been further west than Arkansas.
44. He always wanted to be an arctic explorer.
45. I bought a wooden Noah's Ark for my grandson.
46. So many people are troubled with arthritis as they get older.
47. Mr. Brown will show slides of the artist's work.
48. One might say that lipreading is also an art.

LESSON 40

Words Beginning With aw

Syllables:
    awb–awd–awf–awg–awl–aws–awt–awk

Syllable Drill:

Hōō căn awk
Căn wē awk
Căn wē awb
Căn shē awb
Căn shē awg
Shē căn awg
She can play the organ.

mī gō
hē gō
hē awb
hē awt
wē awt
We ought to go.

Word Drill:

awful	ornate	automatically
awe	order	also
alder	autumn	orderly
August	Austin	organ
awesome	automat	alter
auburn	audition	awning
Albany	alternate	ordeal
awkward	auto	ordinary
always	oration	ought
orchard	austere	organize

Compare:

ād–awd   ēg–awg   īk–awk
awful–lawful   awning–morning
awe–saw   ought–sought
alter–falter   order–border

1. The weather was awful the whole time we were away.
2. There is a black alder in my garden. It has red berries in the autumn.

3. In August there will be a teachers' convention.
4. The snow-capped mountain peaks were an awesome sight.
5. I envy people with auburn hair. It's so pretty.
6. The capital of New York state is Albany.
7. Boys in their teens are apt to be very awkward.
8. Do you always take the turnpike to drive to work?
9. They sell the apples from their large orchard.
10. The Courthouse is very ornate and old-fashioned.
11. Will you please order this list of books for me?
12. I will be glad when autumn comes and the children are in school.
13. We are going to Texas next month to visit my brother in Austin.
14. Have you ever gone to the automat for lunch?
15. She hopes to audition for the opera next spring.
16. I take care of the children on alternate Saturdays.
17. While out for a walk, I didn't hear a car behind me and was nearly hit.
18. His oration was met with enthusiastic cheers.
19. Monks always live a very austere life.
20. They automatically get a raise in wages every two years.
21. We will visit Spain and Portugal, also France.
22. The children filed out of school in an orderly manner.
23. The church is trying to raise money to buy a new organ.
24. Whether she goes with us or not won't alter our plans.
25. A cigarette dropped from an upper window set the awning on fire.
26. Her mother's long illness has been an ordeal.
27. This is no ordinary bird. It's a myna bird and can talk.
28. We ought to be especially careful driving during the holidays.
29. The little boy was very much in awe of the old man.
30. We are going to organize a United Fund in our town.
31. They will alternate the concerts with ballet.
32. We ought to go to the orchard and pick the fruit.
33. The elevators in our building work automatically.
34. Her auburn hair was dressed in a very ornate style.

35. The governor of New York lives in Albany.
36. The examination was an ordeal. It was so difficult.
37. He gives many organ recitals. He is so much in demand.
38. There is an alternate route from here to Boston.
39. The calf was so awkward as he tried to stand on his tall, weak legs.
40. There are always so many auto accidents over the long weekends.
41. My husband is very orderly with his papers and won't have them touched.
42. We always go to my mother's for New Year's.
43. I gave the order for the desks. They ought to be here next week.
44. There was also an awkward situation when the speaker didn't arrive.
45. My car shifts gears automatically.
46. It's awful to have to face such an ordeal.
47. In winter it's an ordinary situation to have many absences from illness.
48. We need some new awnings for the porch.

LESSON 41

Words Beginning With Short ă

Syllables:
ăb—ăk—ăd—ăf—ăg—ăl—ăm—ăp—ăn—ăr—ăs—ăt—ăv—ăz

Syllable Drill:

Wē sā	Hē sō ăg
Hē sā	Hē sī ăz
Hē saw	Hē wī ăf
saw ăk	Hē wō ăd
Hōō ăk	Hē wō ăn
Who saw the accident?	He won't answer.

Word Drill:

am	admire	as
at	allow	ask
add	appear	angry
answer	apt	agree
after	another	accept
ants	attic	absent
ability	an	affair
accident	arrive	address
action	arrest	animal
advice	avenue	adapt

Compare:

ād—ăd	ăz—ēz	āz—ēz
ēt—āt	ōb—ăb	āl—ēl
īr—ār	ĭs—ăs	ăl—ĭl

1. Am I making you understand what I am saying?
2. We will go at once and try to help her.
3. Will you add this column of figures for me? I think I have made a mistake.
4. That is a question I can't answer.
5. After the theater, we went to a nightclub.

Lesson 41

6. I found ants in my bread box when I returned home.
7. The ability to lipread is not easy to achieve.
8. It was an accident that caused his lameness.
9. What action will you take against the boys who broke your fence?
10. I think he gave you good advice. Are you going to take it?
11. We all admire bravery and courage.
12. Will you allow me to take you out to lunch?
13. They don't appear to be very neighborly. They don't speak to anyone.
14. The train is apt to be about fifteen minutes late in the evening.
15. We will have to postpone our trip and go another day.
16. I found this beautiful old vase tucked away in my aunt's attic.
17. An old pair of slippers is so comfortable.
18. I will arrive home in time for dinner on Thursday.
19. Did the police arrest the man, or did he get away?
20. Let's stroll down the avenue and window shop.
21. Agnes and I happened to meet as we were doing our marketing.
22. I will stop the car and you can ask somebody the way to the theater.
23. Please don't be angry with me. I didn't mean to break the dish.
24. I agree completely with your political opinions.
25. I shall accept gratefully your offer of a lift in your car.
26. So many students were absent, they closed the school for a week.
27. How did you hear of the affair? Who told you?
28. I will allow you to borrow the car, but you must be home by twelve.
29. It's good for children to have an animal of their own to care for.
30. Can you adapt the pattern to that material?
31. Please don't ask me to give you an answer today.
32. The film has a great deal of action and is exciting.

33. Her apartment is just off Park Avenue at Seventieth Street.
34. Another time, please ask before borrowing one of my books.
35. The poor little animal was run over by a car.
36. It was an accident and no arrest was made.
37. Can you give me Ann's address in Andover?
38. We are going to add a garage on to the house.
39. I don't think the sun will appear today.
40. Andrew has great ability as a lawyer and has all the work he can do.
41. She is apt to be absent with very little excuse.
42. Will you agree to their proposal?
43. I will answer their note and accept their invitation to dinner.
44. Alec has adapted the words to the music for the show.
45. I was so angry at his action, I couldn't speak.
46. They called from Boston to say they will arrive tomorrow.
47. As I was coming home I passed a terrible accident.
48. Will you give me your new address and telephone number?

LESSON 42

Words Beginning With Short ĕ

Syllables:
    ĕb–ĕk–ĕd–ĕf–ĕg–ĕl–ĕm–ĕn–ĕs–ĕv–ĕt

Syllable Drill:

Wē doo ĕb	sā ĕg
Hoo doo ĕb	thā ĕg
Hoo dĭ ĕb	thā ĕn
How dĭ ĕb	hoo ĕn
How dĭ ĕf	hoo ĕl
How dĭ ĕs	thā ĕl
How did he escape?	They saw the elephant.

Word Drill:

ebb	else	entertain
echo	extra	expert
edge	editor	endless
effort	effect	embrace
egg	element	ever
elbow	emotion	economy
empty	escape	educated
enter	eventually	election
estate	end	electric
every	energy	elephant

Compare:

ĕb–ăb–āb	ĕt–ăt–īt
ĕl–ōl–āl	ĕd–ahd–awd
edge–ledge	end–send
enter–center	egg–beg
effect–defect	edge–hedge

1. The tide is beginning to ebb.
2. Did you ever call out in a cave and hear your voice echo?
3. This knife hasn't got a very sharp edge.
4. It was worth the effort of climbing the hill to see the view.

5. How will you have your egg: boiled, fried or scrambled?
6. I fractured my elbow when I fell on the stone steps.
7. I think I have an empty box that will hold those things for you.
8. Estelle will enter college next fall.
9. They have a very large and beautiful estate on Long Island.
10. Everyone should have some exercise everyday.
11. What else have you to take with you?
12. I'll need an extra hand if I'm going to carry all these books.
13. Did you take the article that you wrote to the editor of the paper?
14. How will this new medicine effect me?
15. His new book has a strong element of suspense to it.
16. Hate is a very strong emotion.
17. It was not easy to escape from Alcatraz.
18. Eventually I mean to sell the house and take an apartment.
19. Isn't it good to see the end of winter nearing?
20. She has so much energy; she is on the go all day long.
21. They entertain a great deal, usually on weekends.
22. I need expert advice in laying out my new garden.
23. The train was so slow, the trip seemed endless.
24. We gave each other a warm embrace. We hadn't met for two years.
25. Did you ever win anything in a raffle?
26. We'll have to practice economy or we will soon be in debt.
27. She is highly educated and holds a very responsible job.
28. Are you pleased with the outcome of the election?
29. Do you use an electric blanket?
30. I wonder why an elephant never forgets?
31. New Year's Day we gave an eggnog party.
32. Let me carry something; I am empty-handed.
33. They say he left his large estate to charity.
34. The way some people elbow their way onto a bus is terrible.
35. Please don't enter without knocking.
36. The Beatles will entertain at a charity ball.

37. It will take expert management to straighten out the company's economy.
38. I wasn't educated to be an economist.
39. Now that the election is over, maybe we can settle down.
40. The new insurance laws will go into effect soon.
41. We must put more effort into raising the money or else we will fail.
42. Have you ever ridden on an elephant?
43. Eventually they will build more housing projects for the elderly.
44. Everyone has so many electric gadgets these days.
45. The train is coming. Keep back from the edge of the platform.
46. Let's go to Florida and escape the cold.
47. Did you ever try to enter politics?
48. Did the lesson seem endless to you? You did well.

LESSON 43

Words Beginning With Short ĭ

Syllables:

    ĭd—ĭf—ĭg—ĭl—ĭm—ĭn—ĭr—ĭt—ĭz

Syllable Drill:

Hōō ĭs ĭl	mā wē ĭm
Hōō ĭd ĭl	mā sō ĭm
Thā ah ĭl	fah sō ĭm
Thā ah ĭn	thā mā ĭm
Thā ah ĭg	mā thā ĭm
They are ignorant.	May they improve?

Word Drill:

if	impair	intrude
idiot	ignorant	irregular
ignore	illusion	is
ill	intend	important
imp	imagine	increase
indeed	in	impossible
improve	income	individual
it	immediately	injure
inch	irritated	ink
imitate	impatient	idiom

Compare:

ĭd—īd—ēd	ĭm—ām—ōōm	ĭl—awl—oul
ill—pill	imp—limp	possible—impossible
it—sit	inch—pinch	tend—intend
ink—drink	ill—fill	rude—intrude

1. I can't fasten your dress if you don't stand still.
2. Only an idiot would go out in this hot sun without a hat.
3. I can't ignore his rudeness to my sister.
4. I went to see my father. He has been ill for a week.

5. The child is an imp, always getting into mischief.
6. It was tragic, indeed, that she lost her only child.
7. The more you practice, the more your lipreading will improve.
8. Here is your ring. I found it on the washstand.
9. Will you please get me a roll of Scotch tape an inch wide?
10. David tries to imitate everything his older brother does.
11. Very noisy working conditions may impair your hearing.
12. The boy was so ignorant he could hardly write his name.
13. When I woke from my dream I had the illusion I was on a ship.
14. Do you intend to apply for the job?
15. I can't imagine where I could have lost my pin.
16. Do you think she has an independent income?
17. They came to help me immediately when I called out.
18. Her ceaseless questions irritated me.
19. Please don't be impatient with me; I am trying to hurry.
20. I didn't mean to intrude. I didn't realize you were not alone.
21. The dress she wore had an irregular hem line.
22. When is the next performance to take place?
23. These papers are important. I will send them registered mail.
24. I have taken a job in order to increase our income.
25. It seems impossible that he didn't notice the theft for a week.
26. She served us individual meat pies for lunch.
27. Did you injure your back in the accident?
28. There is no more ink in my pen. May I borrow yours?
29. The phrase is an idiom of our language.
30. Why did you ignore what I just said to you?
31. I am afraid he will impair our already strained relations with that country.
32. He sometimes acts like an idiot, but he's far from ignorant.
33. They said they would send my order over immediately.
34. It's hard not to be impatient with the children when they whine.

35. My brother is quite ill. We hope his condition will improve soon.
36. The enemy fell back, inch by inch.
37. It's easy to imitate some peoples' mannerisms.
38. The bride wore an illusion veil of white tulle.
39. We are trying to increase our club membership.
40. I am afraid I have spilled some ink on the rug.
41. It's impossible to say if the conference will bring any important change.
42. Every individual has the right to his own opinion.
43. Her business brings her to town at very irregular intervals.
44. I didn't intend to stay longer than two days, but was there a week.
45. It is very rude to intrude on a private conversation.
46. I hope the heavy snow won't injure the shrubs.
47. I imagine my husband will be home before tomorrow night.
48. Irregular practice won't help your lipreading.

LESSON 44

Words Beginning With Short ŭ

Syllables:
        ŭb—ŭg—ŭf—ŭl—ŭm—ŭn—ŭp—ŭs—ŭt

Syllable Drill:

Hōō will ŭb	Thā mā ŭs
Hōō will ŭt	Shē mā ŭs
Thā will ŭt	mā stā ŭs
Thā will ŭn	mā stā ŭp
Will thā ŭn	mā stā ŭn
Will they understand?	She may stay until tomorrow.

Word Drill:

other	usher	ugly
under	about	ulcers
utter	undo	ultimate
until	unfold	oven
unless	understand	up
us	utterly	umbrella
utmost	unusual	uncomfortable
umpire	uncle	upstairs
underwear	unsafe	of
unkind	upon	upper

Compare:

    ăb—ĭb—ŭb   āl—īl—ŭl
    ăs—ĭs—ŭs   ōop—ēp—ŭp
    utter—butter   up—cup
    upper—supper   unkind—some kind
    us—bus   usher—lusher

1. I like the scarf but I think the other goes better with my coat.
2. There are crocus blooming under the tree.

3. I was so frightened I couldn't utter a word.
4. Couldn't you stay until tomorrow?
5. I will stay home today unless my daughter needs me.
6. I must get some underwear for Tommy while the sale is on.
7. She is often unkind and speaks very cuttingly.
8. Will you tell the usher to give us seats further forward?
9. I will be ready to go in about half an hour.
10. Will you undo the zipper of my dress for me, please?
11. Please unfold the tablecloth so that I can see the size.
12. Did you understand what he was trying to tell you?
13. I think their reason for leaving the meeting utterly ridiculous.
14. That is a most unusual brooch. Is it an heirloom?
15. She has gone to England with her uncle.
16. The bridge has been condemned as unsafe.
17. The storm came upon us so suddenly, we hadn't time to take cover.
18. The accident has left him with an ugly scar on his cheek.
19. If you continue to worry, you will end up with ulcers.
20. I think their ultimate goal is worth working for.
21. I will put the roast in the oven now.
22. Have you never been up in a plane? Neither have I.
23. You had better take your umbrella. The sky looks very dark.
24. The brace on his leg looks so uncomfortable.
25. I left my hat and gloves upstairs on the bed.
26. What is the color of your new coat?
27. He knocked out two upper teeth when he fell skating.
28. There is no other way of reaching their farm.
29. I don't think I care to go under the circumstances.
30. The play grew more exciting as the plot unfolded.
31. Practical jokes are often very unsafe.
32. I know he thinks me an utter coward because I'm afraid to fly.
33. Fairy stories always began "Once upon a time."
34. The umpire called "Strike two."
35. They are having to work under difficult conditions.
36. The room was so hot it was like an oven.

37. I hate to take an umbrella; I always leave it somewhere.
38. I will stay here until my brother comes for me.
39. I see I have dropped a stitch. I'll have to undo the last five rows.
40. Unless we get more snow, there will be no skiing.
41. You must drive with the utmost caution when it is stormy.
42. I found a black kitten asleep under my car.
43. We have three rooms and two baths upstairs.
44. Her brother was an usher at her wedding.
45. Unless I hear from you, I will see you tomorrow at six.
46. What other desserts do you have on the menu?
47. It's about time they stopped giving in to the child.
48. The only train accommodation I could get was an upper berth.

LESSON 45

Words Beginning With er—ou—oi

Syllables:

er—urg—ern—irk—erm—urb—urch
our—owl—oun—out
oil—oin—oys

Syllable Drill:

Hōō fō	mī ou hōō
Shē fō	mā ou hōō
Hē fō	thā ou hōō
Hē rou	kă ou hōō
Thē rou	aň ou hōō
Thē ěr	An owl hooted.
The earth is round.	

Word Drill:

urgent	owl	oil
early	out	ointment
earth	our	oyster
erred	ounce	oily
earnest	outcome	
ermine	outdoors	
irk	outrage	
urban	outfit	
urge	outline	
earns	outgrow	

Compare:

earth—birth	owl—fowl	oil—foil
ermine—vermin	out—rout	oily—doily
irk—perk	ounce—pounce	
urge—surge	our—flour	

Lesson 45

1. Mr. Smith, there was an urgent telephone call for you.
2. We had better start early. We have five hundred miles to drive.
3. The earth is not yet warm enough to sow seed.
4. He erred in his estimate of the number of people who would attend.
5. His desire to help us was so earnest.
6. The little girl wore a red coat with an ermine collar.
7. Does it irk you that he is always late?
8. The urban renewal movement is growing in many cities.
9. I urge you not to drive in this weather; it is dangerous.
10. I don't know what salary he earns, but it must be a good one.
11. Sometimes in summer I hear a little hoot owl outside my window.
12. He will be out of the running for a while with his broken leg.
13. Won't you come over to our house? I want to show you the garden.
14. An ounce of prevention is worth a pound of cure.
15. I shall be anxious to hear the outcome of your talk with the governor.
16. We like to cook our dinner on the grill outdoors.
17. It's an outrage the way he takes advantage of his position.
18. Are you getting a new outfit for Easter?
19. I will outline our plan of campaign for you.
20. It is incredible how quickly the children outgrow their shoes.
21. Don't let me forget to buy some salad oil when we are out.
22. Here is some ointment that will help your sunburn.
23. Did you ever open an oyster and find a pearl in it?
24. So many motor boats make the water oily.
25. If you feel the urge to take a walk, I will go with you.
26. The outline of the burglar's shoe was visible under the window.
27. Our club is going to outfit the fife and drum corps.
28. If we get there early, we can probably find seats.

29. A king's robes are always trimmed with ermine.
30. In spite of my diet, I haven't lost an ounce.
31. They got our urgent message and will send us the books tomorrow.
32. The clambake was held outdoors, and they had delicious oyster stew.
33. My car is more than ready for an oil change and lubrication.
34. Mary earns a good salary as a private secretary.
35. I realized that I erred in my judgement of the situation.
36. It seemed to irk the butcher when I spoke of the cost of his meat.
37. The ointment the doctor gave me has healed my burned hand.
38. The speech he made was earnest and to the point.
39. The astronauts must have been so thankful to return to earth.
40. It is too early to know the outcome of the elections.
41. How urgently do you need an accommodation on that plane?
42. An owl always looks so wise.
43. I think little Sally will outgrow her shyness.
44. I can't shake hands. My hands are oily from working with the motor.
45. The baby weighed seven pounds, six ounces.
46. The ever-increasing cost of food is an outrage.
47. I have just finished making an outline for my new book.
48. May I urge you once again to practice your lipreading more.

LESSON 46

s, x and z at the End of a Word

Word Drill:

cliffs	cheese	gracious
knives	daze	pairs
rooms	peas	rinse
farms	please	bees
atlas	pens	plays
cats	ticks	amaze
maps	pots	jazz
sleeps	bottles	packs
carves	jobs	axe
precious	does	delicious
tins	tax	mix
skates	lacks	barks
tires	eggs	box
paints	songs	lose
furs	eats	six
saws	pays	wings
pours	docks	size

Compare:

rinse—rinses	box—boxes
amaze—amazes	tax—taxes
mix—mixes	six—sixes
lose—loses	lack—lacks

1. There were high cliffs on both sides of the river.
2. I gave them a set of steak knives for a wedding present.
3. How many rooms does your apartment have?
4. We passed many prosperous farms as we drove through the country.
5. I don't care for cats; I prefer dogs.
6. An atlas is a book of maps.

7. He always sleeps with his window open, even in winter.
8. Sam carves delightful little figures out of apple wood.
9. Diamonds are a precious stone; a girl's best friend, they say.
10. I always keep crackers in tins so they will stay crisp.
11. Do you want me to take your skates to be sharpened?
12. You will have to get some new tires; yours look very worn.
13. My cousin paints portraits for a living.
14. This shop has beautiful furs. Which do you like, mink or fox?
15. He saws up my firewood for me.
16. What kinds of cheese do you like: swiss, blue or cheddar?
17. I felt I was in a daze, so much had happened so quickly.
18. Do you grow peas in your vegetable garden?
19. I would like some more bread, if you please.
20. There are three pens on my desk; you may borrow one of them.
21. This clock ticks so loudly, I find it annoying.
22. We put up two dozen pots of jam this morning.
23. Many people collect antique bottles.
24. My son does odd jobs for a neighbor on Saturdays.
25. I am afraid the tax on cigarettes is going up again.
26. He who lacks determination will never learn to lipread.
27. Will you pick up a dozen eggs for me at the market?
28. My cleaning woman does a very thorough job.
29. The children love to sit around the camp fire and sing songs.
30. She can never lose weight because she eats so many sweets.
31. He pays the boys very well for the work they do.
32. Martha is always very gracious when asked to help out.
33. I must buy some new stockings. I think I'll get three pairs.
34. You didn't rinse the dishes very well. They are still soapy.
35. There is a lovely cool breeze blowing out on the lawn.
36. Alice plays the piano for the dancing classes.
37. I know it will amaze you to see that our new house is nearly ready.
38. Young Martin plays the sax in a jazz band.
39. He always packs his own bag. He doesn't like it done for him.
40. You will need a good sharp axe to chop that wood.

41. She makes the most delicious cookies I ever ate.
42. Please mix these ingredients while I beat the eggs.
43. My neighbor's dog barks continually.
44. I put six cupcakes in a box for you to take home.
45. A stiff breeze was blowing across the docks when we landed.
46. This morning I watched some baby birds trying their wings.
47. I am sure you know the expression, "It never rains but it pours."
48. This blouse is a little too small. I would like a larger size.

LESSON 47

sh, ch and ge at the End of a Word

Word Drill:

wish	which	urge
cash	rich	age
push	each	page
marsh	reach	rage
fish	peach	cage
dash	march	siege
finish	beach	orange
rush	lunch	college
fresh	touch	passage
clash	church	charge
dish	inch	outrage
harsh	ranch	serge
leash	preach	tinge
splash	teach	change
wash	branch	advantage
lush	starch	splurge

Compare:

wash—washing	age—ageless
rush—rushed	charge—charged
rich—richly	peach—peaches
lunch—lunching	change—changing

1. I wish I could go to the movies with you this evening.
2. Do you wish to charge this, or pay cash?
3. Please push the button so that the elevator will descend.
4. There are many wild ducks in the marsh near my house.
5. We always try to have fish for dinner at least once a week.
6. I will have to dash to the station to catch my train.
7. Do you think you will finish that book this evening?
8. All day long I have had to rush and I'm exhausted.

Lesson 47

9. Please open the window. Let's have a little fresh air.
10. I think these two colors clash. I don't like them together.
11. I'll put a dish of nuts on the bridge table.
12. He had a very harsh voice, very unpleasant to listen to.
13. You had better put the dog on a leash. He will run into the street.
14. Don't walk so near the curb. The cars will splash you.
15. I don't know if it would be best to wash this dress or have it cleaned.
16. The foliage is very lush this year. We have had so much rain.
17. Which car will you buy, the convertible or the hard top?
18. Since he became rich he has no use for his old friends.
19. Each day, I say I will write to Mabel today.
20. We expect to reach Chicago tomorrow.
21. I hate to bite into a peach. The skin feels so furry.
22. There are certainly March winds blowing this morning.
23. A group of teen-agers were sunning themselves on the beach.
24. Lunch will be served at twelve o'clock before the meeting.
25. Please don't touch the cake. It's for dinner tonight.
26. On Sunday, it's difficult to find a place to park near the church.
27. I need a roll of masking tape an inch wide.
28. Her father owns a large ranch in Colorado.
29. This Sunday the Bishop is to preach at our church.
30. I am trying to teach you to lipread.
31. The bank has a branch office on this side of town.
32. The laundry put too much starch in my shirts.
33. I don't want to urge you to go if you don't want to see the show.
34. My cousin's boy is the same age as my son Gerald.
35. Please don't turn down the corner of the page. Use a book mark.
36. My husband was in a rage because Jerry dented the car fender.

37. I will cover the cage for the night so the parrot won't catch cold.
38. They have had a dreadful siege of flu; first one, and then the other.
39. I got some orange-colored drapes for the playroom.
40. He is to take his college boards this week. I hope all will go well.
41. I was lucky to get a passage on the boat at this late date.
42. Edward is in charge of the arrangements for the dinner.
43. The amount they charge in parking garages is an outrage.
44. I like a blue serge suit but they get shiny very quickly.
45. There wasn't even a tinge of color in her face. She was so pale.
46. Do you have change for a dollar? I would like to make a phone call.
47. We have the advantage of living close to the shops.
48. I am going to splurge the ten dollars I won and get a new hair-do.

LESSON 48

Words Ending With t and ed After b, f, v, s, m, p and gh

Word Drill:

night	caught	moved	laughed
exempt	kept	loved	famed
right	doubt	tamed	aped
adopt	leapt	paved	based
eight	bought	carved	camped
light	attempt	loafed	shoved
apt	sight	wrapped	aimed
sought	taught	armed	proved
debt	adapt	rubbed	roamed
slight	thought	claimed	passed
ought	fought	coughed	missed
tight	straight	stabbed	stuffed

Compare:

adopt—adopted keep—kept
move—moved aim—aimed
wrap—wrapped love—loved
rest—rested miss—missed

1. Few doctors will make a house call at night anymore.
2. Roger is exempt from military service because he is deaf.
3. Turn right at the next light and keep on for two blocks.
4. Joan and Andy are going to adopt a little boy.
5. I can't be at your house before eight. Will that be too late?
6. We always leave a light on upstairs when we go out in the evening.
7. We are apt to have a frost any day now.
8. Ships and planes have sought the boat for two days and found nothing.
9. I am afraid the business is heavily in debt.
10. There is slight chance that Bill can get home before Friday.

11. She ought to go and have her hearing tested.
12. These new shoes are a bit tight. I hope they will ease up.
13. I caught four trout on the first day of the fishing season.
14. My cold kept me at home for five days.
15. I doubt that they will be able to sell their house for that price.
16. A big dog leapt at me as I opened the gate.
17. My husband bought me a mink stole for my birthday.
18. I don't think we should attempt the trip until spring.
19. I caught sight of Dick hurrying into the bank.
20. The experience has taught me a lesson.
21. I am sure the child will adapt well to school.
22. I thought you would be home earlier.
23. Our men fought bravely but were heavily out numbered.
24. Walk straight down three blocks and you will come to the church.
25. My brother and his family moved to Chicago last year.
26. She told me she loved to eat artichokes.
27. Have you ever tamed a chipmunk to eat out of your hand?
28. I shall have my driveway paved. It will be easier to plow.
29. Many initials had been carved in the trunk of the old tree.
30. I have loafed for three months; now I must get to work.
31. Please charge the scarf to me, and I would like to have it gift wrapped.
32. They say the escaped criminal is armed and dangerous.
33. I rubbed some liniment into Jack's stiff neck.
34. Nobody has claimed the reward yet.
35. There was a terrible fight and one of the men stabbed the other.
36. I got no sleep last night. I coughed without ceasing.
37. I don't know when I have laughed so much. Our host was so amusing.
38. He is a famed painter and his work is in all the museums.
39. She has and odd way of speaking which is easily aped.
40. The raid was carried out by carrier based planes.

41. We camped in the mountains on our vacation.
42. The crowd was terrible. I was bruised from being elbowed and shoved.
43. He aimed the rifle and shot; the duck dropped to the ground.
44. I think I have proved my point. He agreed to let me go.
45. We roamed the beach picking up shells and driftwood.
46. I passed you yesterday in my car and honked, but you didn't see me.
47. I hope you missed me while I was away.
48. My bag is so stuffed, I can't get another thing in it.

LESSON 49

Words Ending With t and ed After r, l, c, ck

Word Drill:

part	smart	cared	filled
act	tart	stored	fired
start	fort	feared	wired
dirt	pact	failed	smoked
chart	dessert	mailed	lacked
spurt	belt	tucked	tired
report	port	cooled	bored
pert	restrict	pealed	locked
tact	sort	stacked	picked
dart	desert	talked	spelled
distract	cart	called	hired
fact	district	billed	walked

Compare:

    build—built   care—cared
    fall—fault   lock—locked
    tar—tart   stack—stacked
    pack—pact   call—called

1. In what part of town are you looking for an apartment?
2. The government called it an act of aggression.
3. We should start by nine o'clock to reach Boston in time for lunch.
4. The AAA will chart your motor trip for you, if you are a member.
5. Wipe your feet. Don't bring all that dirt into the house.
6. Be careful when you turn on the hose that the water doesn't spurt on you.
7. I didn't hear the weather report on the radio this morning.
8. Alice is a pert little girl and quite charming.

9. Conrad is always putting his foot in his mouth; he has no tact.
10. I can't lipread if there is noise to distract me.
11. The fact is, I can't agree with his way of handling the problem.
12. When school is out, drive carefully; a child may dart into the street.
13. My nephew is very smart and will enter college at sixteen.
14. These tart apples will make a delicious pie.
15. The fort was surrounded by the enemy.
16. The two countries signed a pact of nonaggression.
17. What do you think you would like for dessert?
18. With prices continuing to rise, we will have to restrict ourselves.
19. By which port did you enter the United States?
20. Will you help me to sort these papers and file them?
21. The camel is called the ship of the desert.
22. They gave me a belt with my initials on a silver buckle.
23. The children have a little cart which they love to drag about.
24. In which voting district do you belong?
25. I cared for her house plants while she was away.
26. We have enough firewood stored to carry us through the winter.
27. I feared I wouldn't be home in time to see you before you left.
28. We failed to make our quota for the blood bank.
29. Have you mailed your check for Easter Seals?
30. As soon as I have tucked Tommy in bed we will have dinner.
31. The jam hasn't cooled enough yet to cover the jars.
32. The church bells pealed for service ten minutes ago.
33. I am afraid the cards are stacked against me this evening.
34. We talked on the phone and decided to meet tomorrow at four.
35. I called you five times yesterday, but got no answer.
36. They have billed me already for the shoes I bought last week.
37. Did you have the gas tank filled up before we started?

Alexandria Public Library
Alexandria, Ohio

38. The shop owner fired two clerks last week for laziness.
39. Jean wired that she will not be back until tomorrow.
40. How many cigars have you smoked today?
41. I thought the play lacked originality and was dull.
42. My cousins walked home with me after the movies.
43. I was so bored with the book, I couldn't finish it.
44. Are you sure you locked the car when you parked?
45. We picked up Tom at college on our way home.
46. Do you know how her last name is spelled?
47. They hired a car in Paris and toured through France.
48. That is all for today. I am sure you are tired of concentrating.

LESSON 50

nd and nt at the End of a Word

Word Drill:

bend	send	meant
kind	mind	talent
land	blond	plant
trend	lend	paint
find	band	flaunt
and	fond	present
tend	blind	won't
round	pond	hint
bond	sent	pleasant
found	enchant	bent
mend	can't	accident
sound	couldn't	moment
sand	don't	taunt
end	aunt	faint
rind	lent	mint
brand	saint	dent

Compare:

fine—find   can—can't
ten—tend   could—couldn't
bran—brand   woe—won't
mine—mind   den—dent

1. I will walk as far as the bend in the road with you.
2. What kind of dress are you looking for?
3. We will land tomorrow and I am sorry the voyage is over.
4. The trend seems to be toward co-ed colleges.
5. I can't find my gloves; I must have left them in the car.
6. They say we will have snow and sleet today.
7. I will tend your patient while you get his tray.
8. They have a round mirror hanging over their mantle.

9. The prize was a United States Savings Bond.
10. Their dog was missing for three days, but they have found him.
11. I am going to try to mend this broken vase with cement.
12. Can you hear the sound of the bell when the phone rings?
13. I have so much sand in my shoes, I can't walk.
14. This is a dead-end street. We will have to take the next.
15. These oranges have a very thick rind.
16. What brand of cigarette do you smoke?
17. I hope you will send me a postcard while you are away.
18. Would you mind coming with me to the town hall?
19. I was surprised to see her with red hair. She used to be blond.
20. Please lend me your pen; I forgot to bring mine.
21. I will put an elastic band around these papers so you won't drop any.
22. I am very fond of my aunt. We have always been close.
23. Let me close the blind; the sun is so hot.
24. If you pass a pond or swamp in the spring, you will hear the peepers.
25. I sent Jack and Barbara an invitation to the wedding.
26. I know it will enchant you to see the children's ballet.
27. I can't help wondering what he meant by that remark.
28. Couldn't you join our group on Thursday and go to the fair with us?
29. I don't want to turn in my car until next year.
30. I know Boston well. I have an aunt who lives there.
31. They lent us their boat for the weekend.
32. She is a saint and I think people impose on her.
33. I meant to tell you I had a reassuring letter from her doctor.
34. He paints well, but I don't think he has a great talent.
35. This year I think I will plant petunias in the window boxes.
36. We are going to paint the house in the autumn.
37. She always has to flaunt how many boy friends she has.
38. For the present I am not going to look for another job.
39. I won't be able to keep my appointment at the dentist.
40. Tell me straight out what you want. Don't hint!

Lesson 50

41. The day was so pleasant, and we took a long drive in the country.
42. This nail is too bent; I can't use it. Pass me another.
43. Where and when did the accident happen?
44. For a moment I thought I was going to faint.
45. Don't taunt your sister. You didn't know any better at her age.
46. They made a mint of money with their new venture.
47. There is a dent in the fender of my new car already.
48. Couldn't you try to practice more with different people?

LESSON 51

ng and nk at the End of a Word

Word Drill:

among	gong	thank	prank
stung	young	sink	drunk
long	throng	bank	frank
sang	rang	flunk	rink
wrong	prong	think	sunk
pang	sprung	dank	pink
belong	swung	trunk	brink
rung	along	plank	tank
tongue	flung	link	mink
tang	clung	sank	honk
song	clang	drink	drank
hung	bring	skunk	crank

Compare:

among—amonst honk—honked
belong—belonged link—linking
thank—thankless pink—pinkish
sink—sinking frank—frankly

1. I found your letter among my mail this morning.
2. A huge wasp stung me four times.
3. It's a long road that has no turning.
4. We sat around the campfire and sang old songs.
5. I'm sorry; I think you have the wrong number.
6. A nostalgic pang struck me as I viewed the old house again.
7. The sweater doesn't belong to me. I borrowed it from a friend.
8. His foot slipped on the middle rung of the ladder and he fell.
9. English is not my native tongue.
10. This pear is green and has a very bitter tang.
11. Do you know the old song, "Goodnight Ladies"?
12. I hung the picture you gave me in my living room.

Lesson 51

13. I think I heard the gong for dinner and I'm famished.
14. She isn't working as she has a young child to take care of.
15. There was such a throng at the beach you couldn't even see the sand.
16. The doorbell rang, but when I went to the door nobody was there.
17. I don't know how the prong of this fork got so bent.
18. I have sprung the lock of the door and left my key inside.
19. He swung his golf club but missed the ball.
20. There were daisies growing along the side of the road.
21. When Jack got home, he flung himself onto the divan exhausted.
22. The child clung to his mother. He seemed very shy.
23. I am expecting my cousin next week. May I bring him to see you?
24. We heard the clang of the fire engine as it entered the street.
25. When I see him tomorrow, I will thank him for his help.
26. Just leave the dishes in the sink. I will wash them later.
27. The bank has declared a higher rate of interest on savings.
28. Betty is very worried. She is afraid she will flunk her exam.
29. It's too early to do any planting, but I think I will clean up the yard.
30. My basement is always dank. I can't get it dried out.
31. Will you get my trunk down from the attic, please?
32. Be careful. There is a plank loose on the fourth stair step.
33. I have a broken link in my tire chain. I can hear it clank.
34. The rowboat sank at the dock after the heavy rain.
35. I think you should drink more fluids to help your cold.
36. There was a skunk prowling around last night, and what a smell!
37. It was just a childish prank, but I scolded him.
38. You haven't drunk your coffee; has it become cold?
39. Why can't you be frank with me and tell me what is really bothering you?
40. They have built a new skating rink much bigger than the old one.

41. The boat was sunk by a torpedo.
42. Is pink one of your favorite colors?
43. They are on the brink of disaster. Their firm is doing no business.
44. Your gas tank is only about a quarter full.
45. David gave Angela a mink stole for her birthday.
46. If you honk the horn, they will know we are waiting.
47. He drank thirstily after the long, hot walk.
48. She is a bit of a crank and always complaining.

LESSON 52

tch, ch With the Sound of tch and dge
at the End of a Word

Word Drill:

catch	much	lodge
patch	itch	dodge
pitch	clutch	fudge
switch	twitch	nudge
Welsh	stitch	hedge
match	starch	bridge
crutch	latch	judge
notch	Dutch	badge
stretch	watch	drudge
such	rich	sledge
witch	Scotch	trudge
lunch	edge	cadge
ditch	wedge	budge
punch	ledge	dredge
which	ridge	

Compare:

cat—catch   bad—badge
pit—pitch   sled—sledge
not—notch   cad—cadge
star—starch   dread—dredge

1. Will you help me try to catch my dog?
2. I must patch the hole in this quilt.
3. Didn't you tell me your violin is off pitch?
4. Do you know where the light switch is?
5. My brother just bought a Welsh terrier.
6. Have you a match? My lighter is empty.
7. He has had to use a crutch since the accident.
8. I hope to lose more weight and take up another notch in my belt.

9. If you stretch, you can reach the telephone book for me.
10. It's such a beautiful day! Let's have a picnic.
11. Every Halloween I dress as a witch and fly out on my broomstick.
12. Where do you think you would like to have lunch?
13. I saw the car run off the road into the ditch and turn over.
14. Would you care for another glass of fruit punch?
15. Which of his books did you enjoy most?
16. There isn't much difference in the size of these two dresses.
17. If you put this lotion on your poison ivy, it won't itch.
18. When you shift gears, be sure to throw in the clutch.
19. When you see a dog's leg twitch, you know he is dreaming.
20. What kind of stitch will you use to make the sweater?
21. I would like you to put more starch in my husband's shirts.
22. We should get a new latch for the cabinet. The door keeps opening.
23. Four of us are going to the matinee, Dutch treat.
24. What time does your watch say?
25. This cake is very rich. It's really delicious.
26. I need some Scotch tape to seal this package.
27. I don't know how the edge of this dish got chipped.
28. We will have to wedge the window open; the cord is broken.
29. I saw them sitting on a ledge of rock beside the river.
30. There is a low ridge of mountains behind my house.
31. Would you care to go with us to the ski lodge for the weekend?
32. This is a bad place to cross the street. We will have to dodge the cars.
33. The children love to make fudge on Saturdays.
34. He is a tiresome speaker. Nudge me if I fall asleep.
35. You will recognize the house. It has a low clipped hedge in front.
36. Do you play bridge or poker?
37. The defendant asked the judge for mercy.
38. It is dreadful to have to drudge for a living.

Lesson 52

39. My son has just received his Eagle Scout badge.
40. He has a quick temper but never holds a grudge.
41. The prisoners were breaking up the rocks with sledge hammers.
42. It was a long trudge over the hot, dusty, shadeless road.
43. He is always trying to cadge a drink or a cigarette.
44. My dog wouldn't budge out of my chair even when I tried to sit down.
45. The town is going to dredge the river channel this summer.
46. Please hemstitch the edge of these handkerchiefs.
47. Do you think they will build a bridge over Long Island Sound?
48. I told Jackie if I saw him punch his brother again, I would punish him.

LESSON 53

ing and ic at the End of a Word

Word Drill:

playing	telephoning	traffic
swing	driving	relic
talking	thing	basic
cling	knitting	frolic
dancing	bring	clinic
sling	boasting	attic
sleeping	sing	colic
fling	calling	public
eating	music	chaotic
doing	elastic	erratic
skating	panic	romantic
thinking	tonic	phonetic
sting	plastic	artistic
noticing	comic	realistic
painting	static	caustic
making	cronic	democratic

Compare:

do—doing	pan—panic
make—making	base—basic
call—calling	phone—phonetic
sleep—sleeping	real—realistic

1. The children are playing with their dog.
2. We have a swing hanging from a branch of the apple tree.
3. I was talking to my brother-in-law about vacation plans.
4. I am trying to make the ivy cling to the side of my house.
5. We are going dancing tonight after the show.
6. Would your sore arm feel more comfortable in a sling?
7. My little girl is sleeping, but I will get her up from her nap.
8. Don't fling the newspapers on the floor; put them on the table.

Lesson 53

9. I don't like eating on the beach in the sand.
10. What are you doing tomorrow evening? Could you come to dinner?
11. There is a skating pond only a short distance from where we live.
12. I was thinking of having my living room done over.
13. Be careful, there is a wasp flying around. It may sting you.
14. We were noticing how large the buds on the trees were becoming.
15. Charles bought a painting from me last week.
16. While I was making the beds, the phone rang. It was Jenny.
17. Who were you telephoning to when I came in?
18. My son is having his first driving lesson this afternoon.
19. I am knitting some argyle socks for Donald.
20. I haven't heard a thing about the accident they had.
21. I will bring you some magazines when I come next week.
22. He was boasting about what a gardener he is.
23. Can we persuade you to sing something for us?
24. The children are calling to me to come and see their tree house.
25. Are you fond of music? What kind do you like best?
26. May I put an elastic band around those pamphlets for you?
27. When your hearing aid goes dead, do you panic?
28. Laughter is better than a tonic.
29. These days many children's toys are made of plastic.
30. Do your children read only the comic books?
31. There is something wrong with my radio. I get nothing but static.
32. I think the thing he suffers from most is chronic laziness.
33. The traffic will be very heavy this weekend. Drive carefully.
34. This banner is a relic of my college days.
35. The basic ingredient of the soup is beef and veal.
36. I took the dogs for a long walk and they had a fine frolic.
37. How many times a week do you have to go to the clinic?
38. We are going to clean out our attic and get rid of the junk.
39. I was awake all night. The baby had colic.
40. Let's go for a walk in the public gardens.

41. We moved to our new house today and everything is chaotic.
42. As a worker he is erratic and not very dependable.
43. The old operettas were very romantic.
44. Lipreading is phonetic. You must not think in terms of the alphabet.
45. Jean is very artistic and paints beautiful portraits.
46. You are not being realistic if you think you can make those plants grow.
47. He replied with a very bitter and caustic denunciation of the plan.
48. Do you belong to the Democratic or Republican party?

LESSON 54

ck After Short Vowels and ke After Long Vowels at the End of a Word

Word Drill:

back	sick	cake	poke
shock	stack	like	stake
pick	nick	wake	joke
stock	buck	flake	spike
black	slack	bake	coke
rock	track	quake	spoke
brick	luck	take	lake
dock	trick	brake	dike
quick	pack	shake	fake
sack	duck	choke	bike
block	knock	make	sake
tack	clock	snake	rake

Compare:

    pick—picnic   shake—shaking
    quick—quickly   spoke—spoken
    sick—sickness   joke—joked
    block—blocked   take—taken

1. The doctor told me that I can go back to work Monday.
2. It was a terrible shock to find their home ransacked.
3. I am going to pick some flowers to take to my aunt.
4. We have quite a stock of preserves in our cold cellar.
5. Will you please write the sentence on the blackboard?
6. On a hot summer evening I like to sit on the porch and rock.
7. A brick house is always cooler in summer than wooden ones.
8. We tied up at the Club dock while we went to do some shopping.
9. If you are quick, you can catch the postman. He just left.
10. I must get a sack of lime to put on the lawn.

11. You will block this driveway if you park here.
12. I will tack the notice up on the bulletin board.
13. My cleaning woman called and said she is sick and not coming today.
14. Please stack the wood over against the stone wall.
15. I like this phonograph record. I'm sorry there is a nick in it.
16. I saw a buck and doe run into the woods.
17. This is a slack time of year and many employees are on vacation.
18. It is dangerous to cross the tracks. Take the underground passage.
19. I never have much luck fishing. I'm too impatient.
20. As soon as I pack the picnic lunch, we can start.
21. Do you know a card trick that will amuse us?
22. I thought I heard somebody knock at the door.
23. Do you enjoy duck hunting?
24. I love to hear the grandfather clock strike the hour.
25. The Girl Scouts are having a cake sale on Saturday.
26. Would you like to try this white wine? It is very dry.
27. Please wake me if I oversleep tomorrow morning.
28. The house should be painted. The paint is starting to flake off.
29. They give a clambake for their friends every summer.
30. She was in California at the time of the terrible earthquake.
31. I am going to take the children shopping tomorrow for shoes.
32. Are you sure you put the emergency brake on when you parked?
33. Let's shake the branches; maybe some apples will fall.
34. Bobby took such a large mouthful, I thought he would choke.
35. Would you like to make a date now for your next appointment?
36. When I see a snake, I give it a wide berth.
37. I'll poke the fire and put another log on.
38. We had a new stake put in to hold the mailbox.
39. Bill thought it a great joke that I couldn't get the fish off the hook.
40. A tall spike of hollyhock stood beside the door.

Lesson 54

41. We will need to get some coke for our cookout Sunday.
42. He spoke about his three months stay in Japan.
43. We are taking our new canoe up to the lake this summer.
44. In Holland, if a dike gives way, there is a terrible flood.
45. The painting she bought in Paris turned out to be a fake.
46. Someone stole Dick's bike from the school yard.
47. For your own sake, will you please not work so hard?
48. I have a boy coming to rake the leaves for me this morning.

LESSON 55

nse and nce at the End of a Word

Word Drill:

sense	fence	distance
recompense	bounce	mince
dense	glance	experience
dispense	ounce	acceptance
rinse	dance	lance
tense	sentence	once
pretense	chance	wince
defense	consequence	prance
nonsense	evidence	guidance
offense	romance	balance
response	difference	dunce
expense	since	importance
condense	maintenance	prince
manse	insurance	flounce
tolerance	finance	alliance
entrance	absence	reverence

Compare:

sense—senseless prince—princess
rinse—rinsed finance—financial
offense—offensive expense—expensive
evidence—evident nonsense—no sense

1. I hope the next time you will have more sense.
2. Do you think he will receive a recompense for finding the pin?
3. The fog is so dense, they have closed the airport.
4. Will you dispense the sandwiches while I pour the coffee?
5. I am just going to rinse the dishes and leave them until tomorrow.
6. The crowd was tense watching the flyers jump.

Lesson 55

7. She keeps up a pretense that she likes fishing.
8. They say he shot the man in self-defense.
9. She can talk more nonsense than anyone I know.
10. It's a traffic offense to pass a red light.
11. The response to our appeal has been very heart-warming.
12. To have to buy a new refrigerator now is an unexpected expense.
13. I think the Reader's Digest is planning to condense the book.
14. Some churches call the minister's house the manse.
15. Tolerance is not one of her strongest traits.
16. The entrance to the park is on the other side of the block.
17. A picket fence is nice, but it needs painting so often.
18. I can't seem to bounce back from my bout with the flu.
19. I gave a glance at the weather prediction. It's not very promising.
20. The twins each weighed four pounds, one ounce at birth.
21. Will you be going to the Country Club dance on Saturday?
22. Please repeat the sentence that I have just given you.
23. I only bought one chance in the raffle. I never win anything.
24. As a consequence of his accident, he can't go back to college this term.
25. I don't see any evidence of my tulips coming up yet.
26. Do you prefer to read biographies, or do you like romance?
27. What difference will it make if we are a little late?
28. I hadn't seen Gladys since last 4th of July.
29. We had to sell the boat. We couldn't afford the maintenance.
30. Do you think the man who ran into your car carried insurance?
31. Jack and Arthur are looking for help to finance the venture.
32. They say absence makes the heart grow fonder.
33. You can just see the church spire in the distance.
34. My grandmother used to make delicious mince meat.
35. The canoe trip will be a wonderful experience for the boys.
36. The Johnson's acceptance to the dance came in the mail today.

37. The doctor had to lance the boil on Jim's neck.
38. I wish just once I could get John to cut the grass without arguing.
39. To hear a fork scraped on a dish always makes me wince.
40. My horse hasn't been ridden for three days, so he will prance about.
41. The group is going to Europe under the guidance of the art teacher.
42. Have you ever watched a seal balance a ball on his nose?
43. The boy wouldn't be such a dunce if he would pay attention.
44. I don't know what importance this news has for our government.
45. He is not at all like a prince in a fairy tale.
46. I have torn my dress. I caught my heel in the flounce.
47. We have an alliance with Canada and will never attack each other.
48. Children show little reverence for their parents nowadays.

LESSON 56

**ve and f, gh and ph With the Sound of f
at the End of a Word**

Word Drill:

save	delve	cliff
shove	five	turf
live	olive	puff
solve	above	dwarf
love	dove	sniff
shave	move	deaf
pave	sleeve	leaf
give	grove	muff
dive	life	loaf
glove	bluff	laugh
cave	knife	cough
drive	surf	tough
have	proof	photograph
gave	safe	rough
prove	half	telegraph
leave	calf	autograph

Compare:

    live—living   telegraph—telegram
    have—haven't   safe—saved
    give—gave   leave—leaves
    proof—proven   cough—coughing

1. Do you save trading stamps?
2. I'll just shove these boxes into the closet for now.
3. My mother-in-law is coming to live with us.
4. Do you like to solve mathematical problems?
5. I know she will love the birthday gift you are taking to her.
6. Alfred just went to the barber's for a shave.

7. We have decided to pave our driveway. It will be easier to plow.
8. Will you give me the keys to your car so I can move it?
9. I used to love to dive but now I can't because of my ears.
10. It's so maddening to lose one glove. I'd rather lose the pair.
11. There is so much snow on the flat roof, I'm afraid it may cave in.
12. Will you drive for awhile and let me rest?
13. I have no idea what time it is.
14. I gave her all the paperbacks that I have finished reading.
15. I think I can prove the matter to you.
16. We must leave to go to the boat in about a half-hour.
17. I wish I could stay home and delve into my new book.
18. I'll try to catch the five o'clock train.
19. My new stair carpet is olive green.
20. The Browns live in the apartment above ours.
21. The dove is a symbol of peace.
22. When will the house you are building be ready to move into?
23. I don't know where I picked up this grease spot on my sleeve.
24. Our friends in Florida have an orange grove.
25. Man's life expectancy has been greatly lengthened.
26. Don't try to bluff. I know you haven't even looked at this lesson.
27. If you will fetch me a knife, I will peel this apple.
28. Have you ever tried surfboarding?
29. What proof have you that they will ever pay their debt?
30. The tires on your car don't look safe to me.
31. Almost half the class was absent with colds.
32. The muscles in the calf of my leg are lame from the climb.
33. Don't go near the edge of the cliff; you might fall.
34. There are usually signs on a golf course, "Please replace the turf."
35. A puff of smoke from the cigarette got in my eyes.
36. We planted some dwarf fruit trees.
37. Sniff this rose. Isn't the smell delicious?
38. Hearing people are not very patient with the deaf.

Lesson 56

39. When reading the book, please don't turn down the corner of the leaf.
40. Few women carry a muff these days.
41. Would you pick up a loaf of rye bread for me at the store?
42. Caroline is very witty and she always makes me laugh.
43. That cough you have seems to hang on a long time.
44. I'm afraid you've a very tough problem on your hands.
45. That's a lovely photograph of your mother.
46. The road out to the beach is very rough and stony.
47. I will telegraph to her and ask her to come Saturday instead.
48. Many teen-agers are autograph hunters.

LESSON 57

y With the Sound of ĭ at the End of a Word

Word Drill:

pretty	military	probably
warmly	clearly	study
nicely	weary	naturally
plenty	nearly	obviously
tricky	calmly	many
neatly	destiny	country
jolly	witty	honesty
sharply	salty	durability
hardly	gritty	lucky
valley	pastry	mostly
party	mystery	nasty
agency	utterly	physically
folly	contrary	efficiency
company	duty	affectionately
activity	sultry	coldly
modesty	any	easily

Compare:

neat—neatly men—many
mystery—mysterious near—nearly
acting—activity honesty—dishonesty
paste—pastry agent—agency

1. It will be too warm for a fur coat pretty soon.
2. She greeted me very warmly and made me feel welcome.
3. The child answers very nicely when spoken to.
4. We have plenty of time to catch our train.
5. I'm knitting a sweater and the stitch is a little tricky to do.
6. She dresses her children so neatly. They always look nice.
7. It was a very jolly party they gave last night.
8. He spoke sharply and I could see he was annoyed.

Lesson 57

9. I hardly have time to eat lunch. My appointment is for one o'clock.
10. Do you like the perfume of lilies of the valley?
11. Which political party do you belong to?
12. Perhaps the real estate agency can help you.
13. It's sheer folly to try to make the trip in this storm.
14. They are a large company and manufacture plastics.
15. The children need more activity or they get quarrelling.
16. There's not much modesty left these days.
17. The parade was led by a military band.
18. Can you see me clearly enough to read my lips?
19. Do you feel weary after your long day in town?
20. It's nearly half past five. I must go home and get dinner started.
21. She took it very calmly when the news came that her brother was dead.
22. I guess it's not my destiny to be a lucky winner.
23. He is very witty and makes a very good after-dinner speech.
24. This soup is too salty for my taste.
25. When the windows are open, everything feels gritty from the dust.
26. Do you enjoy French pastry, or do you find it too rich?
27. I am an avid reader of mystery stories.
28. It was utterly ridiculous for her to think she could undertake so much.
29. On the contrary, I thought his speech was very firm and to the point.
30. There will be another nurse on duty from three to eleven.
31. The day has been so hot and sultry. I feel exhausted.
32. Have you any idea what day you will be home from your trip?
33. Probably I won't hear from Jim again before he starts home.
34. If my daughter doesn't study harder, I don't think she'll make college.
35. Mary's hair is naturally curly and a lovely shade of gold.
36. She was obviously pleased by the applause she received.

37. There weren't many people at the meeting; only about twenty-five.
38. As soon as the weather is warmer, we will be going to the country.
39. I know I can trust him. His honesty is well-known.
40. I feel doubtful about the durability of this upholstery fabric.
41. The weatherman says it will be mostly cloudy today.
42. My brother goes to the horse races often and is very lucky.
43. I slipped on the ice and got a nasty cut on my knee.
44. Do you think she is physically up to working any longer?
45. His boss complimented him on his efficiency and good judgment.
46. My niece writes to me often and so affectionately.
47. He looked at the boy so coldly, I knew the child was afraid of him.
48. I think we can easily finish the work by four o'clock.

LESSON 58

l and ble at the End of a Word

Word Drill:

level	fell	able
smile	all	capable
several	full	terrible
girl	tall	table
spool	bell	thimble
coal	fall	profitable
stole	roll	changeable
bowl	dull	marble
tool	small	cable
until	bill	nibble
fuel	call	syllable
pool	smell	reliable
whole	fill	unbearable
pale	doll	scramble
tale	I'll	tremble
still	wall	crumble

Compare:

bearable—unbearable   fill—filling
bill—billed   able—unable
I've—I'll   fall—fallen
scramble—scrambled   whole—wholly

1. This floor isn't level. That is why the table wobbles.
2. She has a very warm and winning smile.
3. I am going to spend several days in Philadelphia.
4. My sister has three children, two boys and a girl.
5. Will you buy me a spool of yellow silk thread?
6. Few people in this area heat their homes with coal anymore.
7. The burglar stole our radio, tape recorder and three rings.
8. I picked a bowl of raspberries from the garden this morning.

9. The weather has been dreadful. I thought it would never stop raining.
10. It will be awful if we miss our train connection in Chicago.
11. Our niece will be with us until the end of the month.
12. What kind of fuel do you use to heat your house?
13. We are thinking of building a swimming pool next summer.
14. The whole family is taking a vacation together this year.
15. Her bridesmaids' dresses were a very pale shade of green.
16. The tale he told about being on a hijacked plane seemed incredible.
17. I fell over one of the children's toys. They are always left about.
18. I think that is about all the news I have I can give you.
19. The young couple are full of plans to build a house.
20. It's too bad she is such a tall girl.
21. I think the doorbell just rang. Will you see who it is?
22. The leaves are beginning to fall. Autumn is early this year.
23. If you don't put on the emergency brake, the car may roll.
24. His lecture was so dull. I was awfully disappointed.
25. We have a very small house, but it is all I want to take care of.
26. I haven't received my telephone bill this month.
27. Please call the children in; it's time they washed up for dinner.
28. The smell of the moonflowers in the warm evening air was delicious.
29. You must fill in this form and send it to the above address.
30. I still have a doll that I had as a child.
31. I'll meet you at the station at four-thirty.
32. A stone wall goes all the way around their property.
33. Will you be able to get off from work early on Friday?
34. I was in a terrible state of indecision about making the trip.
35. Marjorie is a very capable housekeeper.
36. I bought a dining room table and four chairs at the sale.
37. The sewing club gave me a silver thimble as a going-away gift.

Lesson 58

38. They run a very profitable little music shop.
39. The weather is so changeable, one day warm, the next cold.
40. Marble top tables are in style now.
41. We threw the stranded sailboat a cable and towed them free.
42. You shouldn't nibble between meals.
43. Please work harder on your syllable drills.
44. My old car is none too reliable. I should get rid of it.
45. Don't let the dog scramble over you. His paws are muddy.
46. Why do you tremble like that? Are you having a chill?
47. You can crumble this bread and throw it out to the birds.
48. I hope the pain in your hand is not unbearable.

LESSON 59

ion—(sh)ion at the End of a Word

Word Drill:

union	position	devastation
relation	conversation	transportation
pension	billion	provocation
section	oration	devotion
station	division	tuition
scallion	junction	affection
mention	tradition	injection
caution	illusion	irritation
tension	occasion	provision
duration	question	satisfaction
million	direction	objection
motion	combination	auction
vacation	region	nation
demonstration	occupation	situation
attention	religion	education
operation	stallion	television

Compare:

caution—cautioned   question—questioned
mention—mentioned   objection—objected
motion—motionless   station—stationary
region—regional   occasion—occasional

1. The union is going to order a teamsters strike.
2. Is Catherine a relation of yours?
3. The firm gives its employees a very good pension.
4. In what section of the city do you live?
5. The station was so crowded with children leaving for camp.
6. I think I'll put a scallion or two in the salad.
7. The weather bureau didn't mention rain for today.
8. May I caution you to start early; the traffic will be very heavy.

Lesson 59

9. A hearing problem causes a person much tension.
10. We had a bad thunderstorm yesterday, but of short duration.
11. The new museum is to cost over a million dollars.
12. Does the motion of a ship make you feel seasick?
13. I haven't yet decided where I will go on my vacation this year.
14. The artist gave a demonstration of painting at the museum.
15. In order to learn to lipread, you must give your full attention.
16. My aunt had an operation this spring and her recovery is slow.
17. Charles has just accepted a new position with an electronics firm.
18. Are you able to join in a conversation with more than one person?
19. I can't even think of the figure five billion, four hundred million.
20. We expected him to make an oration, but he spoke very briefly.
21. We are going to make a division of the property into two acre lots.
22. The accident happened at the junction of routes fifty-four and nine.
23. It's a family tradition that the same veil be worn by each bride.
24. I had the illusion that I was going to find the work easy.
25. We went to a party on Saturday. The occasion was a twenty-fifth anniversary.
26. I don't think I quite understand the question.
27. Which direction are you going? Perhaps I could go with you?
28. We are having a combination birthday and christening party.
29. That region of the country is very mountainous.
30. It's not good to be idle. Everyone should have an occupation.
31. Some people get more comfort from their religion than others.
32. My uncle just bought a beautiful stallion for his horse farm.
33. Forest fires have caused terrible devastation in California.

34. Do you need transportation to the polling place?
35. He is ready for a fight at the least provocation.
36. John shows such devotion to his wife and children.
37. At some schools for the handicapped, the tuition is necessarily high.
38. I wish Natalie would show more affection for her father.
39. You should get an injection for your hay fever.
40. It's hard not to show irritation when people don't face you when speaking.
41. I have laid in a good provision of meat in my freezer.
42. When you discover that you can lipread, it is a great satisfaction.
43. Have you any objection to my borrowing these books?
44. We went to an auction on Saturday. I bought some china.
45. They are a nation of peace loving people.
46. The situation is difficult because the working conditions aren't good.
47. I don't think she has ever had much education.
48. Do you watch televsion or do you flnd it frustrating?

LESSON 60

er—or—ar at the End of a Word

Word Drill:

paper	razor	bar
after	tailor	pillar
butter	candor	car
wonder	furor	poplar
chatter	harbor	far
better	clamor	dollar
ladder	arbor	jar
hammer	corridor	caviar
fender	dissenter	mar
needier	aviator	collar
darker	commuter	tar
father	objector	popular
later	director	star
manner	color	cellar
sitter	doctor	scar
caterer	endeavor	beggar

Compare:

color—colorless   wonder—wonderful
needier—needless   objector—objection
chatter—chattering   director—directing
darker—darkness   aviator—aviation.

1. I am afraid they forgot to leave us the morning paper.
2. It was a nice evening and after dinner we went for a walk.
3. Do you mind eating oleo on your toast or would you rather have butter?
4. I wonder if my tulips will come up. The bulbs seemed small.
5. I never knew anyone who could chatter as much as Connie.
6. Now that the weather is better we can take some drives.

7. Would you hammer these hooks in and hang the pictures for me?
8. I don't think my ladder is tall enough to reach the apples.
9. I think I have set a record. I have had the car a year without a dent.
10. We will see that these clothes are given to some of the needier people.
11. She is looking for a rug for her living room, a darker shade of blue.
12. Frank's father is a senator.
13. Later on we can make more definite plans.
14. Dorothy has a very warm manner and always makes you feel at home.
15. I'm trying to get a baby sitter for Saturday evening.
16. Do you know of a good caterer we could get to do the party?
17. I have to stop at the drugstore and pick up some razor blades for Jim.
18. You had better take those trousers to the tailor and get them shortened.
19. She answered me with complete candor when I asked her how she felt.
20. The children were making such a furor, I didn't hear the bell.
21. There were many boats in the harbor for the regatta.
22. Stop making such a clamor; you will each get your balloon.
23. The roses on the arbor are in full bloom.
24. Don't leave boxes in the corridor where people will fall over them.
25. When we asked who wanted to go for a picnic, there wasn't a dissenter.
26. Her brother was an aviator in World War II.
27. This town has a large commuter population.
28. I think Albert is a conscientious objector.
29. He is very young to be a museum director.
30. These pansies are such a lovely color.
31. I expect the doctor will come to see Bob this morning.

Lesson 60

32. Please endeavor to come to the meeting. We need all the support we can get.
33. All I had for lunch was a chocolate bar.
34. There was a red rose climbing up the pillar of the porch.
35. In France many country roads are lined with poplar trees.
36. How far did you go on your hike Saturday?
37. I can't go to market today. I only have a dollar in my purse.
38. I haven't a single jar of jam left on my pantry shelf.
39. They had all sorts of canapes at the cocktail party, including caviar.
40. You will mar the surface of the table if you put that wet glass down.
41. Turn up the collar of your coat so the rain won't go down your neck.
42. The sun is so hot that the tar on the road is melting.
43. Do you like classical or popular music?
44. Did you ever wish on a star?
45. The cellar is so damp, I must open the door and let the air dry it.
46. How did you get the long scar on your arm?
47. If you dent the fender of my car I will be very angry.
48. There was a beggar going from door to door, so I notified the police.

LESSON 61

less and ness at the End of a Word

Word Drill:

hopeless	endless	drabness
useless	colorless	generousness
meaningless	tasteless	dampness
heartless	penniless	tartness
aimless	thoughtless	happiness
thankless	speechless	distinctness
homeless	powerless	calmness
painless	tactless	sickness
careless	unless	thankfulness
faultless	business	goodness
groundless	kindness	rudeness
dauntless	promptness	firmness
pitiless	likeness	newness
formless	softness	sweetness
timeless	tenderness	faintness
doubtless	madness	dryness

Compare:

thoughtless—thoughtlessness   careless—carelessness
hopeless—hopelessness   tactless—tactlessness

1. I am afraid it is hopeless to go on hunting for the plane.
2. Don't you think it useless to keep the old, broken chair?
3. To me the book was trite and meaningless.
4. She is a very heartless person and thinks only of herself.
5. Frank always seems to interest himself in the most aimless projects.
6. Trying to keep this big, old house clean is a thankless job.
7. A homeless cat has attached himself to me. I want to get rid of him.
8. Getting a flu shot is painless.

Lesson 61

9. The gardener I have is very careless with his tools.
10. She speaks faultless French and Spanish.
11. I am sure your fears for Caroline are groundless.
12. My nephew Nick is a dauntless mountain climber.
13. Professor Green is pitiless when it comes to giving out homework.
14. Kate is tireless in her efforts to raise money for the Red Cross.
15. The Sphinx seems to hold a timeless message.
16. Doubtless you will be taking your vacation soon.
17. The play bored me and it seemed endless.
18. My garden did poorly this year and is quite colorless.
19. Don't you find the food very tasteless in this restaurant?
20. We heard she'd been left penniless; her husband had only debts.
21. It was very thoughtless of me not to have offered her a lift.
22. We were struck speechless when he told us the news.
23. Dick said he was powerless to get the firm to take Bill on.
24. Mildred is always tactless. If only she'd think before she speaks.
25. We are going to the ball game tomorrow unless it rains.
26. What type of business is your husband in?
27. I couldn't thank them enough for their kindness when I was stranded.
28. I hate to wait for people; I appreciate promptness.
29. Curt is the portrait painter I would choose. He gets a good likeness.
30. Just feel the softness of this blanket, and it's so light.
31. It's madness to think you can drive all that distance in one day.
32. She shows her little blind sister a great deal of tenderness.
33. The drabness of some cities in winter is very depressing.
34. Her generousness knows no bounds; she would give you anything she had.
35. All the dampness we have had makes my arthritis ache.
36. The tartness of these apples make them perfect for pie.

37. Father gets a great deal of happiness out of being with his grandchild.
38. Grace's distinctness of speech makes her a good teacher.
39. We should all try to show calmness in a crisis.
40. There has been a lot of sickness this winter, more than usual.
41. Her thankfulness was evident when she heard that she needed no operation.
42. For goodness sake, where have you been all this time?
43. Her children's rudeness doesn't seem to bother her at all.
44. If Doris would show more firmness with the boy, he wouldn't be in trouble.
45. The kids are thrilled at going to school, but wait until the newness is over.
46. The child's sweetness charmed everyone.
47. A feeling of faintness came over me, the room was so awfully hot.
48. I think the dryness of the mountain air will help your sinus.

LESSON 62

ful at the End of a Word

Word Drill:

hopeful	sinful	wistful
tearful	fearful	delightful
dreadful	powerful	bashful
awful	pitiful	wonderful
mindful	doubtful	rightful
doleful	chock-full	boastful
sorrowful	meaningful	mournful
trustful	harmful	handful
careful	purposeful	beautiful
armful	cheerful	mouthful
thoughtful	shameful	wasteful
tactful	thankful	healthful
playful	merciful	restful
willful	watchful	gleeful
joyful	colorful	cupful
wishful	youthful	frightful

Compare:

dreadful—dreadfully   shameful—shamefully
awful—awfully   cheerful—cheerfully
careful—carefully   beautiful—beautifully
willful—willfully   frightful—frightfully

1. We are hopeful that Jim will be able to walk again eventually.
2. Her loss is so recent, she is still in the tearful stage.
3. Isn't it dreadful the number of accidents that occur on holidays?
4. We have an awful bunch of bills to pay this month.
5. Are you being mindful of the time? We musn't be late.
6. What a doleful day this is, no sun and so chilly.

7. Naturally we are sorrowful over her leaving us.
8. The puppy is so trustful and friendly, always wanting attention.
9. Please be careful going down these stairs; the lighting isn't good.
10. I will appreciate a lift. This armful of books weights a lot.
11. It was most thoughtful of you to send me the newspaper article about Jo.
12. Joyce is always so tactful and kind.
13. The new kitten I got is all black and so playful.
14. Julia is the most willful child I have ever seen.
15. Everyone was joyful over the good news.
16. Hoping for a reduction in taxes, I am afraid, is wishful thinking.
17. Wasting good food is really sinful.
18. I never knew anyone so fearful of trying something new as Amy is.
19. Jacob is a powerful swimmer and is on the Olympic team.
20. Her longing to take part in the activities of other children is pitiful.
21. Because of the storm, it is doubtful that the boat will dock tomorrow.
22. Do you ever buy Chockfull O' Nuts coffee? I have never tried it.
23. I think the article he wrote on housing was meaningful and helpful.
24. Diving can be harmful to your ears. You should wear ear plugs.
25. The club's meetings are purposeful and they have accomplished good work.
26. Barbara enjoys good health and she is always cheerful and gay.
27. The litter in the streets is absolutely shameful.
28. I am so thankful the weather is cooler.
29. What a merciful escape they had when the truck struck their car.

Lesson 62

30. A good baby sitter should be watchful and alert.
31. The floats in the parade were very colorful.
32. Don't you think he is very youthful for his age?
33. Ann is a very wistful child. I'm afraid she is too sensitive.
34. The Browns have a delightful small house on Cape Cod.
35. Chris is very bashful and it makes him stutter.
36. We had a wonderful day at the World's Fair, but it was exhausting.
37. The ring you found should be returned to its rightful owner.
38. Don't you hate people who are boastful and noisy?
39. The sound of the foghorn out in the bay was mournful.
40. Mary and Bill have five children. They are certainly a handful.
41. I envy her the beautiful roses she has in her garden.
42. You have scarcely eaten a mouthful. Aren't you hungry?
43. To be wasteful is bad management.
44. They say it's healthful to drink milk.
45. May I sit for awhile in your garden? It's so restful and quiet.
46. The children were gleeful that school was over for the summer.
47. Does the recipe call for one cupful of celery, or two?
48. We had a frightful thunderstorm last night. Did you get it too?

LESSON 63

ld and lt at the End of a Word

Word Drill:

bold	cold	knelt
field	gold	bolt
sold	hold	quilt
child	scold	salt
told	bolt	wilt
scald	guilt	halt
fold	melt	jolt
shield	built	malt
mold	silt	spilt
build	dealt	vault
mild	fault	tilt
held	felt	belt
bald	dwelt	kilt
old	jilt	colt
yield	pelt	hilt

Compare:

bold—boldly molt—molting
guilt—guilty hold—holding
fault—faulty pelt—pelting
salt—salty wilt—wilting

1. The girl was very bold and answered me impudently.
2. There is a big field near our house where my dog loves to run.
3. Have you sold your house, or have you taken it off the market?
4. I found the child wandering in the street and took him to the police.
5. Nick told me they expect to go to Greece in October.

6. Be careful not to knock over that pot of boiling water. You would be scalded.
7. Will you help me to fold these sheets so that I can put them away?
8. I am going to put up the beach umbrella to shield us from the sun.
9. You could make an aspic mold and fill it with shrimp salad.
10. I believe they are going to build a new hospital.
11. This cheese is very mild. I think you will like it.
12. Joseph held the horse's head while I mounted.
13. They say wearing a hat indoors makes a man bald.
14. My aunt is very old. She is ninety-three.
15. We hope our fruit trees will yield a better crop this year.
16. How did you catch such a dreadful cold?
17. My uncle gave me a gold bracelet.
18. Will you hold these books while I look in my bag for the keys?
19. Please don't scold me. I didn't mean to be late.
20. I always bolt the doors of the house at night.
21. She had a feeling of guilt because she lost her engagement ring.
22. The sun is so hot, it's making the pavement melt.
23. A catbird has built a nest right beside my door.
24. There was a lot of silt in the bath water. The pipes need flushing.
25. I dealt last. It's Frank's deal.
26. It wasn't your fault that the electricity went off and you couldn't cook.
27. My mother felt the heat and humidity dreadfully.
28. She dwelt on one subject for so long, I thought she'd never finish.
29. You can't be afraid that Tom is going to jilt you.
30. A skunk's pelt always smells when it is wet.
31. She knelt beside the boy and tried to comfort him until help came.
32. I can't lock the door; the bolt is stuck.

33. There was a beautiful patchwork quilt shown at the fair.
34. It's extremely difficult to stay on a salt-free diet.
35. The flowers I picked this morning are beginning to wilt already.
36. They are trying to halt the spread of the epidemic.
37. Don't jolt the tray. You will make me spill the soup.
38. Come with me to the drugstore. I'm dying for a chocolate malt.
39. The baby spilt his milk all over the rug.
40. I must go to the safe deposit vault at the bank this morning.
41. If you tilt your chair so far back, you will go over.
42. She wore a brightly striped belt with her white dress.
43. A Scotchman wears a kilt.
44. The boy romped in the field with the colt.
45. The gold hilt of the sword was beautifully etched.
46. The bank has built a new vault, two floors below the ground.
47. I must fold this quilt and put it away for the summer.
48. Grandfather wants his hat. He says his bald head feels cold.

LESSON 64

st and ft at the End of a Word

Word Drill:

toast	yeast	lift
trust	dust	soft
most	boost	sift
thrust	rust	left
boast	coast	rift
moist	lost	tuft
list	crust	aft
nest	post	loft
past	just	craft
blast	mist	shift
cast	last	draft
jest	fist	shaft
mast	vast	theft
gust	raft	gift
must	swift	thrift

Compare:

most—mostly swift—swiftly
dust—dusty soft—softly
mist—misty craft—crafty
gust—gusty thrift—thrifty

1. I'm afraid I have burned the toast. The toaster was set too high.
2. I trust you have learned a lesson and won't make the same error again.
3. Most of our delphinium were winterkilled.
4. The child thrust the bunch of flowers at me and ran.
5. If my garden was as beautiful as yours, I would boast about it.
6. You must keep the ground moist around the evergreens.

7. Here is the grocery list. Will you pick up these things for me?
8. The boys found a bird's nest and brought it home.
9. In the past we used to get snow much earlier.
10. A blast of the auto horn told me a car was coming around the bend.
11. George taught me to trout fish and cast a fly.
12. It was meant to be a jest but it fell flat.
13. I snapped off the mast of my car radio aerial.
14. A gust of wind blew the sand into my eyes.
15. We must find time to go to Jerome's exhibition.
16. Yeast is used in the making of beer.
17. The galloping horses threw up the dust.
18. I'm afraid they are going to boost the taxes again this year.
19. We will have to scrape the rust off the railing before we can paint it.
20. There have been very high tides all along the coast.
21. Julia has lost a lot of weight and looks much better.
22. You make a much better pie crust that I do.
23. May I post that letter for you? I'm going right by the mailbox.
24. We will be able to see the Statute of Liberty in just a few minutes.
25. The mist was very heavy on the water this morning.
26. The last time I saw Kevin was New Year's Day.
27. Don't pound your fist on the table.
28. The Sahara desert is very vast.
29. I understand he hit his head on the raft while diving.
30. I felt like giving him a swift kick for his impudence.
31. Will you lift the books off the table so that I can put this tray down?
32. Do you prefer chocolates with soft centers or chewy with nuts?
33. I am going to sift this earth for potting soil.
34. At the traffic light, should I turn left or right?
35. Another rift has occurred in the diplomatic relations between the countries.

36. A daisy has a tuft of yellow in the center.
37. I went aft to sit with my husband at the tiller.
38. Do you know how to loft a kite?
39. It is a good thing to learn a craft to have as a hobby.
40. Do you have a stick shift on your car or automatic transmission?
41. I feel a draft around my legs. I think someone left the door open.
42. Have you ever been down a mine shaft?
43. The theft of your hi-fi must be a blow to you.
44. They received a gift of silver dollars as an anniversary present.
45. Trying to teach my daughter thrift seems hopeless.
46. Their boat is a small sailing craft.
47. I trust Jacob to look after the house when we go away.
48. Jimmy thrust his fist in his pocket and pulled out some marbles.

LESSON 65

us and ous at the End of a Word

Word Drill:

minus	capricious	enormous
furious	anxious	contagious
cautious	gracious	obvious
jealous	luscious	mischievous
devious	dubious	nervous
copius	conscious	marvelous
pretentious	gorgeous	notorious
advantageous	numerous	mountainous
dangerous	envious	studious
continuous	glorious	courageous
tedious	victorious	luxurious
obnoxious	sinus	precious
courteous	ambitious	delicious
laborious	joyous	curious
various	tempestuous	luminous

Compare:

gracious—graciously curious—curiously
anxious—anxiously luxurious—luxuriously
obvious—obviously furious—furiously
cautious—cautiously dangerous—dangerously

1. Is that last figure plus or minus the total?
2. I was furious that I was too late to get tickets for the show.
3. It is best to be cautious when trying the ice on a pond.
4. Mary's twin, Mike, is very jealous of her boy friends.
5. You had better remember that that man is very devious in his dealings.
6. We had a copious rainfall last week. It did the garden good.
7. Don't you think their house on Long Island very pretentious?
8. The shop had a very advantageous sale. I got several bargains.

Lesson 65

9. The astronauts undertake very dangerous missions.
10. We have had three weeks of continuous heat.
11. They said the drive across the desert was very tedious.
12. Some weeds have a most obnoxious smell.
13. The clerks at Brown's Store are always most courteous.
14. The climb up the mountain was laborious and the going slow.
15. I have various errands to do this morning and will have lunch out.
16. Jane is so capricious; she never sticks to anything.
17. Of course, we are very anxious to have Don come home.
18. Dorothy is a very gracious hostess.
19. These pears are luscious, so juicy.
20. I think it is dubious whether they will be able to make the trip.
21. I wasn't conscious of the slip he made.
22. The sunset last night was gorgeous. We watched until the sun was gone.
23. I received numerous phone calls asking to look at the house.
24. I am so envious of your beautiful peonies.
25. What a glorious day! Shall we go for a picnic?
26. The home team returned victorious.
27. This dry atmosphere is very bad for sinus trouble.
28. Martin is very ambitious. I think he will go far.
29. We had a joyous Christmas with all the family together.
30. The sea looks very tempestuous this morning.
31. Gladys baked an enormous cake for the birthday party.
32. Measles and mumps are very contagious.
33. It was obvious that she didn't mean to tell me the whole story.
34. Mary Ann is the most mischievous child I have ever run into.
35. Were you nervous the first time you were up in a plane?
36. It was a marvelous ball the Greens gave last night.
37. Walter is notorious for his luck at the horse races.
38. They are afraid the plane must have come down in a mountainous region.
39. I certainly wish my daughter was as studious as yours.
40. She is so courageous in spite of all the troubles she has had.

41. The new University Club is very luxurious.
42. Which of the precious stones is your favorite, diamonds or sapphires?
43. This dessert is delicious. Where did you learn to make it.
44. I was curious to know who she heard the story from.
45. It's very starry tonight and the Milky Way is very luminous.
46. I shall be anxious about the children until I know they have arrived.
47. The road through the mountains is very dangerous.
48. Weeding the garden is laborious and very tiresome.

HOMOPHENOUS SOUNDS

HOMOPHENOUS WORDS

Alexandria Public Library
Alexandria, Ohio

HOMOPHENOUS SOUNDS

f–v–ph–gh–(laugh)
m–b–p–mb–mp
w–wh–(qu)
s–z–soft c
sh–ch–j–soft g
d–t–n–nt–nd
k–hard c–hard g–nk–ng

HOMOPHENOUS WORDS

aim–ape
art–hard–heart
armed–harmed
aground–around
all–hall–haul

bar–mar–par
bull–pull
beak–meek–peak
bound–pound–mound
black–blank–plank
bride–bright–pride
braid–brain–prayed
beach–peach
bill–mill–pill
bush–push
beer–mere–pier

could–good
crowd–crown–crowned–ground
cite–side–sign
chop–shop
class–glass

crime–grime–gripe
cold–gold
crab–cram–cramp–grab
case–gaze
chair–share
cab–camp–cap–gap
come–cup–gum
card–cart–guard
chews–choose–juice–shoes
chipped–shipped
cheat–sheet
chose–shows
choice–joys

dim–dip–nip–tip
dumb–dump–numb–tub
dine–nine–tine
dime–time–type
die–tie
doesn't–dozen
done–none–ton–nut
dry–try–dried–tried
drain–train–trade–trait

dame—name—tame—tape
dear—near—tear
doze—knows—toes
drip—trip—trim
drew—true

erred—heard
ear—here—year
eyes—ice

firm—verb
falls—false
face—phase—vase
few—view
fine—vine
fade—fate
friend—fret

gild—gilt—guilt—killed

laid—lain—late
lack—lag—lank
lamb—lamp—lap

limb—limp—lip
lad—land
loom—loop

meal—peal—peel
mood—moon
may—pay—bay

need—neat
nail—tail—tale
niece—knees

plaid—planned
pies—buys
penny—many

roam—robe—rope
read—red—rend—rent—wren
root—route—rude
recite—reside—resigned
rack—rag—rang—rank
ride—right

sea—see
sad—sand—sat

sick—sing—sink
sack—sag—sang—sank
strain—straight—strayed
sheep—cheap
shows—chose
shame—shape
smoke—spoke
stain—state—stayed
shop—job
swear—square
summer—supper

thawed—thought
thumb—thump
thick—thing—think
throat—thrown

wade—wait—wane—weight
wide—wine—whine—white
wear—where

zoo—sue